THE ABU GHRAIB INVESTIGATIONS

THE ABU GHRAIB INVESTIGATIONS

*The Official Reports
of the Independent Panel and
Pentagon on the Shocking
Prisoner Abuse in Iraq*

———————

EDITED BY STEVEN STRASSER

With an Introduction by Craig R. Whitney

PublicAffairs
New York

Published in the United States by PublicAffairs™,
a member of the Perseus Books Group.

Book design and composition by Mark McGary
Set in Sabon

ISBN 1-58648-319-6

FIRST EDITION
10 9 8 7 6 5 4 3 2 1

Contents

INTRODUCTION

Craig R. Whitney

The photographs did not lie.

American soldiers, male and female, grinning and pointing at the genitals of naked, frightened Iraqi prisoners; an Iraqi man, unclothed and leashed like a dog, groveling on the floor in front of his female guard; a prisoner standing on a box with a sandbag over his head and wires attached to his body beneath a poncho. These were not enemy propaganda pictures; these showed real atrocities actually inflicted by Americans.

Those pictures, the first of which were broadcast on the CBS program *60 Minutes II* in the spring of 2004 showed that much had gone terribly wrong in Iraq, but more than dismay, they inspired revulsion. Whatever they thought about the Bush administration's reasons for going to war, most Americans believed that Iraq and the world were better off without Saddam Hussein and his torturers. Now here was evidence that only a year later in Abu Ghraib, one of Saddam's cruelest prisons, Americans, too, were torturing Iraqi civilians.

It was only an aberration, Americans were quickly assured by the military and civilian officials who had led them into the war. Like drunken participants in a fraternity party, rogue soldiers, some of them reservists who were prison guards in civilian life, had violated official Pentagon policies, U.S. Army doctrine, and standard procedures for handling prisoners. Investigations had long been under way, justice would be done. Soon Pfc. Lynndie R. England, Specialist Charles A. Graner Jr., Staff Sgt. Ivan L. Frederick II, and four other military police soldiers, like them all of enlisted rank, were facing court-martial charges of committing assault, mistreatment, and sexual abuse of prisoners—violations of the laws of war.

The seriousness of the crimes was beyond argument. The damage to the reputation of the United States in the world and to the reputation of American forces in Iraq was incalculable, as was the threat to the security of those forces from the swelling ranks of anti-occupation insurgents. In the international furor, President Bush said he was sorry "for the humiliation suffered by Iraqi prisoners and the humiliation suffered by their families," but rejected calls for the resignation of Secretary of Defense Donald H. Rumsfeld, who visited Iraq in May and swore, "The people who engaged in abuses will be brought to justice."

War, any war, as an American World War II hero, Gen. Omar N. Bradley, wrote, was "a wretched debasement of all the thin pretensions of civilization." Yet decent people had tried, as modern weaponry had made death and mayhem on the battlefield ever more horrific, to contain the uncontrollable. The nations of the world had established the Red Cross and Red Crescent and tried to codify limits to permissible violence in agreements called Geneva Conventions, starting in 1864. They were strengthened again after the unimaginable slaughter of World War I, yet had no effect on preventing equally unimaginable Nazi and Japanese atrocities during World War II. In reaction to the horrors of the Holocaust and the brutalities of Axis POW camps, the United States and most of the rest of the world agreed to four Geneva Conventions in 1949 prescribing basic minimal protections for soldiers, sailors, prisoners of war and civilians caught up in war, providing among other things that none should be subjected to physical or mental torture or to cruel or degrading corporal punishment.

The Geneva Conventions had been observed in the breach by North Korean and Chinese forces during the Korean War. In Vietnam, both North and South Vietnam tortured prisoners, when they took any at all, and John S. McCain III and other U.S. POWs suffered for years in the Hanoi Hilton. But the United States had learned its lessons from Vietnam, Americans were assured by their leaders, and had gone to war in Iraq to defend civilized values, not to destroy them. The abuses at Abu Ghraib threw that basic assumption of decency into doubt. So now the people in whose name the war was being fought demanded to know who was responsible.

Not since Lt. William L. Calley Jr. had led 25 men from the Americal Division into the central Vietnamese hamlet of My Lai in 1968 and systematically gunned down 150 unarmed old men, women, and children had Americans felt such reason to question the fundamental decency of American troops in wartime. Lieutenant Calley's men had been deranged by a long war few of them understood, among civilians it was impossible for them to tell from the enemy as they stumbled into minefields, living in daily fear of being picked off in ambushes by the Vietcong guerrillas who found shelter and sympathy in the impoverished villages. The war had ground on even with half a million troops in Vietnam, nearly all of whom could not communicate with the people they had been sent to defend. Soldiers were sent into villages on search and destroy missions against an enemy who could turn out to be any civilian or child they came across. At night, the troops huddled in bases as artillery fired rounds into "free fire zones" where no Vietnamese was safe.

In such a climate of fear and confusion, some officers were not up to the task of leadership. Lieutenant Calley and his platoon ran wild in My Lai on that March day in 1968. But a courageous American helicopter pilot, Warrant Officer Hugh Thompson, saw what was going on and stopped the violence by threatening to open fire on Calley and his men. Other soldiers reported the atrocities to their superiors, whose initial reaction was to cover up the crimes. Eventually, after the journalist Seymour M. Hersh broke the story, charges were brought and 12 officers were court-martialed for dereliction of duty. Of those, one general was reduced in rank; another was censured. The rest were either acquitted or had the charges against them dismissed.

Lieutenant Calley and a dozen other officers and enlisted men were tried for war crimes, but only one guilty verdict was returned, against Calley for the murder of 22 unarmed civilians. His life sentence was later reduced to 10 years, and in 1974 Calley walked free on parole. My Lai became a front in the other Vietnam war, the one that divided Americans so profoundly about their country's involvement and about their own participation in it. A young Navy lieutenant named John Kerry spoke at a Senate hearing in 1971 of "the absolute horror" many Vietnam veterans felt about "what this country, in a sense, made them do." Others felt resentful of this attitude and cheated of the pride of serving their country after the communists won in 1975. These divisions opened again during the presidential election campaign of 2004.

Nightmares long suppressed after Vietnam began recurring after Abu Ghraib, where, as with My Lai, decent American troops appalled by seeing other soldiers abuse prisoners reported their crimes to their superiors. This time, higher authority took action. Army investigators began a criminal inquiry into individual abuses in the fall of 2003, though the public did not learn what they had found until after the pictures surfaced the following April.

Ultimately, the investigations had implications that extended all the way up the chain of command to the White House—implications their findings make clear but not always explicit.

The initial Army criminal inquiries' results were so troubling that in January 2004, Lt. Gen. Ricardo S. Sanchez, the overall military commander in Iraq, appointed a high-level investigator, Maj. Gen. Antonio M. Taguba, to determine the responsibilities farther up the chain of command. General Taguba widened the inquiry to include the entire 800th Military Police Brigade, commanded by Brig. Gen. Janis L. Karpinski, and the 372nd MP Company of the brigade's 320th MP Battalion, the guard unit in charge of Abu Ghraib. The entire brigade, General Taguba found, was inadequately trained for its mission, with "a general lack of knowledge, implementation, and emphasis of basic legal, regulatory, doctrinal and command requirements." Most of the soldiers in the brigade had expected to go home after American forces occupied Baghdad in the spring of 2003 and were demoralized when they were kept on into the fall to handle an influx of thousands of detainees from the gathering insurgency against the occupiers, who had been assured by Washington that they would be welcomed with open arms.

At the prison, which was often under mortar attack

from the insurgents, procedures for identifying and handling detainees were chaotic. The military police were overwhelmed. They were also confused about the lines of authority between themselves and the Military Intelligence soldiers and CIA civilians who were interrogating prisoners for information about the insurgents. "MI [military intelligence] wanted to get them to talk," a female MP soldier testified; MPs did their bidding by softening them up in ways some of them thought were allowed by rapidly shifting rules on handling detainees.

General Taguba found instances of illegal and intentional abuse of detainees by the military police, including keeping prisoners naked for days at a time; forcing them to masturbate while being photographed and videotaped; placing a dog chain around a prisoner's neck and photographing him next to a female guard; and using dogs without muzzles to intimidate and frighten prisoners, and in one case to bite and severely injure one. Taguba recommended disciplinary action and further investigation against a dozen officers and civilians, none higher in rank than General Karpinski, and a further investigation of Military Intelligence to determine its share of responsibility for the abuses.

A separate inquiry began on the role intelligence soldiers had played. It was led initially by Maj. Gen. George R. Fay and later, when General Sanchez himself had to be questioned, by Lt. Gen. Anthony R. Jones.

Their final reports drew a picture of the reality that had produced the aberrations at Abu Ghraib, a reality that had many similarities to the morass Lieutenant Calley and his men had fallen into at My Lai, one created in part by decisions in Washington. Secretary of Defense Rumsfeld had overridden the recommendations of his Army advisers even before the war in Iraq began and insisted that the military conduct combat operations with far fewer soldiers than many officers thought necessary. The deputy defense secretary, Paul D. Wolfowitz, had called "wildly off the mark" an estimate by Gen. Eric K. Shinseki, then the Army chief of staff, that several hundred thousand troops would be needed to occupy Iraq after the war was over; the Pentagon expected things to calm down and planned for only about 100,000.

But when resistance to the occupation surged and uprisings began in the late summer and fall of 2003, the occupiers were overwhelmed. At Abu Ghraib, by October there were 7,000 prisoners bursting the prison walls, but only 92 military police guards to keep them under control. Instead of a grateful Iraqi civilian population, "leaders and soldiers confronted a faceless enemy whose hatred of the United States knew no limits," as General Jones wrote in his report. In such an environment, General Fay found, disorganization, inadequate leadership and poor supervision worked to produce an attitude of fear and sullen resentment among the guards and interrogators at Abu Ghraib.

Lt. Col. Steven L. Jordan, who was in charge of the interrogation center at the prison, and ten other soldiers had been wounded and two soldiers were killed in a mortar attack on Abu Ghraib in September of 2003, and frequent mortar attacks followed all winter, culminating in one in April 2004 that killed 22 prisoners and wounded 80 others. "The soldiers' and civilians' morale at Abu Ghraib suffered as the attacks continued," General Fay wrote. "Additionally, there was a general feeling by both MI and MP personnel that Abu Ghraib was the forgotten outpost receiving little support from the Army." The lines of authority between Military Police guards and Military Intelligence and CIA and other civilian interrogators were confused and poorly understood.

Only "a small group of morally corrupt and unsupervised soldiers and civilians" had committed sexual and physical abuse under these chaotic conditions, General Fay found, but he noted, "The climate created at Abu Ghraib provided the opportunity for such abuse to occur and to continue undiscovered by higher authority for a long period of time." He found numerous incidences of abuse by military intelligence soldiers during interrogations and recommended administrative actions, not court-martials, for Colonel Jordan and the 205th Military Intelligence Brigade commander, Col. Thomas M. Pappas, and other officers.

General Jones endorsed those findings, but also addressed a further issue, one that lay at the heart of what had gone wrong at Abu Ghraib. This was the confusion that President Bush and Secretary of Defense Rumsfeld had introduced into the issue of handling prisoners when the administration decided in late 2001 and early 2002 that members of Al-Qaeda and of the Taliban captured in Afghanistan in the war on terrorism that began after Sept. 11 were not entitled to be considered prisoners of war as defined by the Geneva Conventions. Instead, they were to be considered "unlawful combatants" who, whether as detainees in the highly secretive U.S. facility at Guantanamo Bay or elsewhere, fell under rules the administration alone would prescribe. Detainees were to be "treated humanely and, to the extent appropriate and consistent with military necessity, in a matter consistent with the principles of Geneva," the president had decided, but both the secretary of defense and General Sanchez would at different times authorize exceptions to the normal prisoner-handling rules. Legal memoranda prepared by the Justice Department in the period leading up to the president's decision seemed to show an administration seeking justification in law for torture. Though this was denied, it would soon become clear that the president's decision had far-reaching consequences.

"Had Army doctrine and training been followed, the abuses at Abu Ghraib would not have occurred," General Jones noted in his report, emphasizing that there was no excuse for the soldiers who did not follow them. But there were explanations, and his report offered several of them. In December 2002, Mr. Rumsfeld's office had authorized interrogation techniques for "unlawful combatants" in Afghanistan and Guantanamo, including the use of dogs to induce stress and the removal of clothing to break down detainees' resistance to questioning, and later rescinded and revised the rules. General Sanchez himself had issued several policy memos on treatment of prisoners in Iraq to put greater pressure on them to provide information on insurgent activities that could save the lives of American soldiers, then revised the memos in ways that left the rules vague.

Though the harsh techniques allowed at Guantanamo and in Afghanistan were never meant to apply to prisoners in Iraq, General Jones found, "some military intelligence personnel executing their interrogation duties at Abu Ghraib had previously served as interrogators in other theaters of operation," including Afghanistan and Guantanamo. "Therefore, the existence of confusing and inconsistent interrogation technique policies contributed to the belief that additional interrogation techniques were condoned in order to gain intelligence," the Jones report said.

Further confusion was caused by the presence of CIA and perhaps other secret government interrogators operating under their own rules at Abu Ghraib, General Fay's report found. Their more lax procedures "eroded the necessity in the minds of soldiers and civilians for them to follow Army rules." The door was thus open, in weaker minds, to treat prisoners in ways that included "cases of clothing removal (without any touching), some use of dogs in interrogations (uses without physical contact or extreme fear), and some instances of improper imposition of isolation," General Jones found. None of these techniques authorized by President Bush or Secretary Rumsfeld had ever authorized sexual abuse or physical violence against prisoners, his report said, but the confusion in General Sanchez's own memoranda had "led indirectly to some of the non-violent and non-sexual abuses," in General Jones's words.

In such a morally ambiguous climate, under stress, rotten apples among the guards on the night shift at Abu Ghraib went further. If all the normal rules no longer apply, those inclined to brutality may feel that anything goes. General Sanchez, like the president and the secretary of defense, could not be held responsible for those. And so the weight of military justice fell on Private England, Specialist Graner, and the other low-ranking soldiers who had clearly committed illegal acts in Abu Ghraib, and on junior officers and enlisted men in Navy Seal and other Special Forces Units charged with similar offenses in Afghanistan.

But there was a relationship, nonetheless, between abstract political acts by high officials in Washington and illegal actions by simple soldiers in Baghdad. That much was clear from the report of the Independent Panel to Review DoD Detention Operations, headed by former Secretary of Defense James R. Schlesinger, which Mr. Rumsfeld commissioned in the spring of 2004 to determine "the cause of the problems and what should be done to fix them," not only in Abu Ghraib but elsewhere.

The Independent Panel issued its report and recommendations in August, finding 66 cases substantiated by that time, eight in Guantanamo, three in Afghanistan and 55 in Iraq, one third of them (including five detainee deaths) during interrogations. The shocking abuses in the photographs, the forced masturbation, and the gratuitous violence committed "just for the fun of it," the panel found, had not occurred during intelligence questioning but "would have been avoided with proper training, leadership and oversight."

The occupation forces in Iraq faced a situation in which standard procedures for rounding up prisoners on the battlefield and detaining them in the rear areas were inadequate. In the Independent Panel's words, in Iraq "there are no safe areas behind 'friendly lines'—there *are* no friendly lines." Abu Ghraib was dysfunctional from the start, the panel observed: "The choice of Abu Ghraib as the facility for detention operations placed a strictly detention mission-driven unit—one designed to operate in a rear area—smack in the middle of a combat environment."

In this environment, intelligence and military police commanders felt pressure to obtain information that could help save the lives of American soldiers, pressure even from the White House, which sent a senior member of the National Security Council Staff to Abu Ghraib in November 2003. "Despite the number of visits and the intensity of interest in actionable intelligence, however, the Panel found no undue pressure exerted by senior officials. Nevertheless, their eagerness for intelligence may have been perceived by interrogators as pressure," the Independent Panel found.

The more serious question was whether U.S. military observance of international conventions on the law of war had been degraded in the minds of soldiers whose duty was to observe them in Iraq. "Although specifically limited by the Secretary of Defense to Guantanamo, and requiring his personal approval (given in only two cases), the augmented techniques for Guantanamo migrated to Afghanistan and Iraq where they were neither limited nor safeguarded," the Independent Panel found. The Guantanamo commander, Maj. Gen. Geoffrey Miller, was sent to Iraq by the Pentagon in August 2003 to assess interrogation and detention operations there, and as later congressional hearings put it, the prison operations were "Gitmo-ized," with prison guards assigned the responsibility of "preparing the conditions" for successful interrogations of prisoners—softening them up, in other words, for the interrogators.

He "brought the Secretary of Defense's April 16, 2003 policy guidelines for Guantanamo with him and gave this policy to [General Sanchez] as a possible model for the command-wide policy that he recommended be established," the panel reported, though General Miller noted that it applied only to unlawful combatants at Guantanamo and not in Iraq. Nevertheless, in the panel's findings, General Sanchez did authorize a dozen interrogation techniques beyond those permitted by standard Army doctrine, and though he later rescinded that authorization, in the ensuing confusion some soldiers in the field came to believe that harsher techniques were condoned. And a few apparently concluded that all the wraps on torture were off.

Nowhere, perhaps, has the law of unintended consequences ever had more demonstrable effects than in Iraq. Yet, in Washington, State Department and Joint Chiefs of Staff lawyers had foreseen some of them, warning the administration early on that declaring that Geneva Conventions did not apply to Al-Qaeda or Taliban prisoners could come back to haunt policymakers. "They were concerned that to conclude otherwise would be inconsistent with past practice and policy, jeopardize the United States armed forces personnel, and undermine the United States military culture which is based on a strict adherence to the law of war," the Independent Panel noted.

These State Department and Pentagon lawyers had been prescient. Under pressure, in the chaos of combat, distinctions like the one the president made, excepting those prisoners from Geneva Convention protections but ordering them to be treated in a way that was consistent with such protections, could be and were easily lost—just as distinctions were lost between rules that applied only in Afghanistan or Guantanamo and rules intended for Iraq.

Only the soldiers who actually committed the abuses of physical and mental torture bore direct responsibility for them, the Independent Panel found. But its own findings laid indirect responsibility for some of the abuses at the door of the Pentagon and the White House, the details of whose policy on the rights of detainees the panel found "vague and lacking." That policy, it concluded, needed to be defined "in a way consistent with U.S. jurisprudence and military doctrine and with U.S.

interpretation of the Geneva Conventions," the same way for the CIA and other government agencies as for the military.

The lack of postwar planning that left military personnel so understaffed and demoralized at Abu Ghraib was also the fault of senior officials, the Independent Panel found. At one point, General Sanchez had only 495 of the 1,400 people he needed to run his operational headquarters in Iraq, it reported: "We note, however, in terms of its responsibilities, [his command] was never fully resourced to meet the size and complexity of its mission," a failure for which the panel did not explicitly hold authorities in Washington personally responsible.

"The damage these incidents have done to U.S. policy, to the image of the U.S. among populations whose support we need in the Global War on Terror and to the morale of our armed forces, must not be repeated," the Independent Panel concluded.

Many Americans felt, as the administration did after Sept. 11, that terrorists bent on inflicting civilian casualties deserved no quarter. Senator Joseph Biden of Delaware reminded administration officials at a hearing in June 2004 that one reason Americans accept international treaties on the rights of prisoners of war is "so when Americans are captured, they are not tortured." Treaties may have little meaning for non-state entities like al Qaeda, but if the United States disregards their provisions for other adversaries, there is little reason to hope that they will be honored for Americans. The "laws of war" may be an oxymoron, but debasing those laws puts everyone who wears the uniform in peril.

That is why soldiers are being prosecuted for prisoner abuse that disgraced that uniform and their hundreds of thousands of fellow soldiers who served honorably in Iraq. But like Lieutenant Calley, the enlisted guards in Iraq on whom the consequences of military justice seemed likely to fall most heavily drew sympathy and support from some who believed they were scapegoats. They faced heavy jail terms if convicted. As for their superior officers, some were relieved of command, some were reprimanded and had their careers cut short, but none seemed likely to go to prison. There were other investigations, including one involving more than two dozen soldiers involved in the deaths of two detainees in Afghanistan even before the war in Iraq, and several inquiries by the CIA into its own interrogation practices. The war against terror, in Iraq and elsewhere, would continue.

The electorate would make its own judgment on November 2, 2004, on what responsibility should be borne by those who made the political and policy decisions that led, indirectly or not, to the aberrations at Abu Ghraib.

FINAL REPORT OF THE
INDEPENDENT PANEL TO REVIEW
DEPARTMENT OF DEFENSE
DETENTION OPERATIONS

———

FINAL REPORT OF THE INDEPENDENT PANEL TO REVIEW DEPARTMENT OF DEFENSE DETENTION OPERATIONS

———

Chairman
The Honorable James R. Schlesinger

———

Panel Members
The Honorable Harold Brown
The Honorable Tillie K. Fowler
General Charles A. Homer (USAF-RET)

———

Executive Director
Dr. James A. Blackwell, Jr.

OVERVIEW

The events of October through December 2003 on the night shift of Tier 1 at Abu Ghraib prison were acts of brutality and purposeless sadism. We now know these abuses occurred at the hands of both military police and military intelligence personnel. The pictured abuses, unacceptable even in wartime, were not part of authorized interrogations nor were they even directed at intelligence targets. They represent deviant behavior and a failure of military leadership and discipline. However, we do know that some of the egregious abuses at Abu

Ghraib which were not photographed did occur during interrogation sessions and that abuses during interrogation sessions occurred elsewhere.

In light of what happened at Abu Ghraib, a series of comprehensive investigations has been conducted by various components of the Department of Defense. Since the beginning of hostilities in Afghanistan and Iraq, U.S. military and security operations have apprehended about 50,000 individuals. From this number, about 300 allegations of abuse in Afghanistan, Iraq or Guantanamo have arisen. As of mid-August 2004, 155 investigations into the allegations have been completed, resulting in 66 substantiated cases. Approximately one-third of these cases occurred at the point of capture or tactical collection point, frequently under uncertain, dangerous and violent circumstances.

Abuses of varying severity occurred at differing locations under differing circumstances and context. They were widespread and, though inflicted on only a small percentage of those detained, they were serious both in number and in effect. No approved procedures called for or allowed the kinds of abuse that in fact occurred. There is no evidence of a policy of abuse promulgated by senior officials or military authorities. Still, the abuses were not just the failure of some individuals to follow known standards, and they are more than the failure of a few leaders to enforce proper discipline. There is both institutional and personal responsibility at higher levels.

Secretary of Defense Donald Rumsfeld appointed the

members of the Independent Panel to provide independent professional advice on detainee abuses, what caused them and what actions should be taken to preclude their repetition. The Panel reviewed various criminal investigations and a number of command and other major investigations. The Panel also conducted interviews of relevant persons, including the Secretary and Deputy Secretary of Defense, other senior Department of Defense officials, the military chain-of-command and their staffs and other officials directly and indirectly involved with Abu Ghraib and other detention operations. However, the Panel did not have full access to information involving the role of the Central Intelligence Agency in detention operations; this is an area the Panel believes needs further investigation and review. It should be noted that information provided to the Panel was that available as of mid-August 2004. If additional information becomes available, the Panel's judgments might be revised.

POLICY

With the events of September 11, 2001, the President, the Congress and the American people recognized we were at war with a different kind of enemy. The terrorists who flew airliners into the World Trade Center and the Pentagon were unlike enemy combatants the U.S. has fought in previous conflicts. Their objectives, in fact, are to kill large numbers of civilians and to strike at the heart of America's political cohesion and its economic and military might. In the days and weeks after the attack, the President and his closest advisers developed policies and strategies in response. On September 18, 2001, by a virtually unanimous vote, Congress passed an Authorization for Use of Military Force. Shortly thereafter, the U.S. initiated hostilities in Afghanistan and the first detainees were held at Mazar-e-Sharrif in November 2001.

On February 7, 2002, the President issued a memorandum stating that he determined the Geneva Conventions did not apply to the conflict with Al-Qaeda, and although they did apply in the conflict with Afghanistan, the Taliban were unlawful combatants and therefore did not qualify for prisoner of war status. Nonetheless, the Secretary of State, Secretary of Defense, and the Chairman of the Joint Chiefs of Staff were all in agreement that treatment of detainees should be consistent with the Geneva Conventions. The President ordered accordingly that detainees were to be treated "... humanely and, to the extent appropriate and consistent with military necessity, in a manner consistent with the principles of Geneva." Earlier, the Department of State had argued the Geneva Conventions in their traditional application provided a sufficiently robust legal construct under which the Global War on Terror could effectively be waged. The Legal Advisor to the Chairman, Joint Chiefs of Staff, and many of the military service attorneys agreed with this position.

In the summer of 2002, the Counsel to the President queried the Department of Justice Office of Legal Counsel for an opinion on the standards of conduct for interrogation operations conducted by U.S. personnel outside of the U.S. and the applicability of the Convention Against Torture. The Office of Legal Counsel responded in an August 1, 2002 opinion in which it held that in order to constitute torture, an act must be specifically intended to inflict severe physical or mental pain and suffering that is difficult to endure.

Army Field Manual 34–52, with its list of 17 authorized interrogation methods, has long been the standard source for interrogation doctrine within the Department of Defense. In October 2002, authorities at Guantanamo requested approval of stronger interrogation techniques to counter tenacious resistance by some detainees. The Secretary of Defense responded with a December 2, 2002, decision authorizing the use of 16 additional techniques at Guantanamo. As a result of concerns raised by the Navy General Counsel on January 15, 2003, Secretary Rumsfeld rescinded the majority of the approved measures in the December 2, 2002, authorization. Moreover, he directed the remaining more aggressive techniques could be used only with his approval.

At the same time, he directed the Department of Defense General Counsel to establish a Working Group to study interrogation techniques. The Working Group was headed by Air Force General Counsel Mary Walker and included wide membership from across the military legal and intelligence communities. The Working Group also relied heavily on the Office of Legal Counsel. The

Working Group reviewed 35 techniques and after a very extensive debate ultimately recommended 24 to the Secretary of Defense. The study led to the Secretary of Defense's promulgation on April 16, 2003, of a list of approved techniques strictly limited for use at Guantanamo. This policy remains in force at Guantanamo.

In the initial development of these Secretary of Defense policies, the legal resources of the Services' Judge Advocates General and General Counsels were not utilized to their full potential. Had the Secretary of Defense had a wider range of legal opinions and a more robust debate regarding detainee policies and operations, his policy of April 16, 2003, might well have been developed and issued in early December, 2002. This would have avoided the policy changes which characterized the December 2, 2002, to April 16, 2003, period.

It is clear that pressures for additional intelligence and the more aggressive methods sanctioned by the Secretary of Defense memorandum resulted in stronger interrogation techniques that were believed to be needed and appropriate in the treatment of detainees defined as "unlawful combatants." At Guantanamo, the interrogators used those additional techniques with only two detainees, gaining important and time-urgent information in the process.

In Afghanistan, from the war's inception through the end of 2002, all forces used Field Manual 34–52 as a baseline for interrogation techniques. Nonetheless, more aggressive interrogation of detainees appears to have been ongoing. On January 24, 2003, in response to a data call from the Joint Staff to facilitate the Working Group efforts, the Commander Joint Task Force–180 forwarded a list of techniques being used in Afghanistan, including some not explicitly set out in Field Manual 34–52. These techniques were included in a Special Operations Forces Standard Operating Procedures document published in February 2003. The Military Intelligence Battalion, a company of which was later sent to Iraq, assisted in interrogations in support of Special Operations Forces and was fully aware of their interrogation techniques.

Interrogators and lists of techniques circulated from Guantanamo and Afghanistan to Iraq. During July and August 2003, the 519th Military Intelligence Company was sent to the Abu Ghraib detention facility to conduct interrogation operations. Absent any explicit policy or guidance, other than Field Manual 34–52, the officer in charge prepared draft interrogation guidelines that were a near copy of the Standard Operating Procedure created by Special Operations Forces. It is important to note that techniques effective under carefully controlled conditions at Guantanamo became far more problematic when they migrated and were not adequately safeguarded.

Following a request by CJTF–7 [Combined Joint Task Force 7, the forward-deployed military headquarters in Iraq], Joint Staff tasked the Southern Command to send an assistance team to provide advice on facilities and operations, specifically related to screening, interrogations, human intelligence collection, and inter-agency integration in the short and long term. In August 2003, Maj. Gen. Geoffrey Miller arrived to conduct an assessment of Department of Defense counterterrorism interrogation and detention operations in Iraq. He was to discuss current theater ability to exploit internees rapidly for actionable intelligence. He brought the Secretary of Defense's April 16, 2003, policy guidelines for Guantanamo with him and gave this policy to CJTF–7 as a possible model for the command-wide policy that he recommended be established. Major General Miller noted that it applied to unlawful combatants at Guantanamo and was not directly applicable to Iraq, where the Geneva Conventions applied. In part as a result of Major General Miller's call for strong, command-wide interrogation policies and in part as a result of a request for guidance coming up from the 519th at Abu Ghraib, on September 14, 2003 Lt. Gen. [Ricardo] Sanchez [commander of CJTF–7] signed a memorandum authorizing a dozen interrogation techniques beyond Field Manual 34–52— five beyond those approved for Guantanamo.

Major General Miller had indicated his model was approved only for Guantanamo. However, CJTF–7, using reasoning from the President's Memorandum of February 7, 2002 which addressed "unlawful combatants," believed additional, tougher measures were warranted because there were "unlawful combatants" mixed in with Enemy Prisoners of War and civilian and criminal detainees. The CJTF–7 Commander, on the advice of his

Staff Judge Advocate, believed he had the inherent authority of the Commander in a Theater of War to promulgate such a policy and make determinations as to the categorization of detainees under the Geneva Conventions. Central Command viewed the CJTF–7 policy as unacceptably aggressive and on October 12, 2003, Commander CJTF–7 rescinded his September directive and disseminated methods only slightly stronger than those in Field Manual 34–52. The policy memos promulgated at the CJTF–7 level allowed for interpretation in several areas and did not adequately set forth the limits of interrogation techniques. The existence of confusing and inconsistent interrogation technique policies contributed to the belief that additional interrogation techniques were condoned.

Detention And Interrogation Operations

From his experience in Guantanamo, Major General Miller called for the military police [MP] and military intelligence [MI] soldiers to work cooperatively, with the military police "setting the conditions" for interrogations. This MP role included passive collection on detainees as well as supporting incentives recommended by the military interrogators. These collaborative procedures worked effectively in Guantanamo, particularly in light of the high ratio of approximately 1 to 1 of military police to mostly compliant detainees. However, in Iraq and particularly in Abu Ghraib the ratio of military police to repeatedly unruly detainees was significantly smaller, at one point 1 to about 75 at Abu Ghraib, making it difficult even to keep track of prisoners. Moreover, because Abu Ghraib was located in a combat zone, the military police were engaged in force protection of the complex as well as escorting convoys of supplies to and from the prison. Compounding these problems was the inadequacy of leadership, oversight and support needed in the face of such difficulties.

At various times, the U.S. conducted detention operations at approximately 17 sites in Iraq and 25 sites in Afghanistan, in addition to the strategic operation at Guantanamo. A cumulative total of 50,000 detainees have been in the custody of U.S. forces since November 2001, with a peak population of 11,000 in the month of March 2004.

In Iraq, there was not only a failure to plan for a major insurgency, but also to quickly and adequately adapt to the insurgency that followed after major combat operations. The October 2002 Central Command War Plan presupposed that relatively benign stability and security operations would precede a handover to Iraq's authorities. The contingencies contemplated in that plan included sabotage of oil production facilities and large numbers of refugees generated by communal strife.

Major combat operations were accomplished more swiftly than anticipated. Then began a period of occupation and an active and growing insurgency. Although the removal of Saddam Hussein was initially welcomed by the bulk of the population, the occupation became increasingly resented. Detention facilities soon held Iraqi and foreign terrorists as well as a mix of Enemy Prisoners of War, other security detainees, criminals and undoubtedly some accused as a result of factional rivalries. Of the 17 detention facilities in Iraq, the largest, Abu Ghraib, housed up to 7,000 detainees in October 2003, with a guard force of only about 90 personnel from the 800th Military Police Brigade. Abu Ghraib was seriously overcrowded, under-resourced, and under continual attack. Five U.S. soldiers died as a result of mortar attacks on Abu Ghraib. In July 2003, Abu Ghraib was mortared 25 times; on August 16, 2003, five detainees were killed and 67 wounded in a mortar attack. A mortar attack on April 20, 2004 killed 22 detainees.

Problems at Abu Ghraib are traceable in part to the nature and recent history of the military police and military intelligence units at Abu Ghraib. The 800th Military Police Brigade had one year of notice to plan for detention operations in Iraq. Original projections called for approximately 12 detention facilities in non-hostile, rear areas with a projection of 30,000 to 100,000 Enemy Prisoners of War. Though the 800th had planned a detention operations exercise for the summer of 2002, it was cancelled because of the disruption in soldier and unit availability resulting from the mobilization of Military Police Reserves following 9/11. Although its readiness was certified by U.S. Army Forces Command, actual deployment of the 800th Brigade to Iraq was chaotic. The "Time Phased Force Deployment List," which was the planned flow of forces to the theater of operations, was scrapped in favor of piecemeal unit deployment orders based on actual unit readiness and personnel strength. Equipment and troops regularly arrived out of planned sequence and rarely together. Improvisation was the order of the day. While some units overcame these difficulties, the 800th was among the lowest in priority and did not have the capability to overcome the shortfalls it confronted.

The 205th MI Brigade, deployed to support Combined Joint Task Force 7, normally provides the intelligence capability for a Corps Headquarters. However, it was insufficient to provide the kind of support needed by CJTF–7, especially with regard to interrogators and interpreters. Some additional units were mobilized to fill in the gaps, but while these MI units were more prepared than their military police counterparts, there were insufficient numbers of units available. Moreover, unit cohesion was lacking because elements of as many as six different units were assigned to the interrogation mission at Abu Ghraib. These problems were heightened by friction between military intelligence and military police personnel, including the brigade commanders themselves.

ABUSES

As of the date of this report, there were about 300 incidents of alleged detainee abuse across the Joint Operations Areas. Of the 155 completed investigations, 66 have resulted in a determination that detainees under the control of U.S. forces were abused. Dozens of non-judicial punishments have already been awarded. Others are in various stages of the military justice process.

Of the 66 already substantiated cases of abuse, eight occurred at Guantanamo, three in Afghanistan and 55 in Iraq. Only about one-third were related to interrogation, and two-thirds to other causes. There were five cases of detainee deaths as a result of abuse by U.S. personnel during interrogations. Many more died from natural causes and enemy mortar attacks. There are 23 cases of detainee deaths still under investigation: three in Afghanistan and 20 in Iraq. Twenty-eight of the abuse cases are alleged to include Special Operations Forces and, of the 15 Special Operations Forces cases that have been closed, ten were determined to be unsubstantiated and five resulted in disciplinary action. The Jacoby review of Special Operations Forces detention operations found a range of abuses and causes similar in scope and magnitude to those found among conventional forces.

The aberrant behavior on the night shift in Cell Block 1 at Abu Ghraib would have been avoided with proper training, leadership and oversight. Though acts of abuse occurred at a number of locations, those in Cell Block 1 have a unique nature fostered by the predilections of the noncommissioned officers in charge. Had these noncommissioned officers behaved more like those on the day shift, these acts, which one participant described as "lust for the fun of it," would not have taken place.

Concerning the abuses at Abu Ghraib, the impact was magnified by the fact the shocking photographs were aired throughout the world in April 2004. Although Central Command had publicly addressed the abuses in a press release in January 2004, the photographs remained within the official criminal investigative process. Consequently, the highest levels of command and leadership in the Department of Defense were not adequately informed nor prepared to respond to the Congress and the American public when copies were released by the press.

POLICY AND COMMAND RESPONSIBILITIES

Interrogation policies with respect to Iraq, where the majority of the abuses occurred, were inadequate or deficient in some respects at three levels: Department of Defense, Central Command/CJTF–7, and Abu Ghraib Prison. Policies to guide the demands for actionable intelligence lagged behind battlefield needs. As already noted, the changes in Department of Defense interrogation policies between December 2, 2002, and April 16, 2003, were an element contributing to uncertainties in the field as to which techniques were authorized. Although specifically limited by the Secretary of Defense to Guantanamo, and requiring his personal approval (given in only two cases), the augmented techniques for Guantanamo migrated to Afghanistan and Iraq, where they were neither limited nor safeguarded.

At the operational level, in the absence of specific guidance from Central Command, interrogators in Iraq relied on Field Manual 34–52 and on unauthorized techniques that had migrated from Afghanistan. On September 14, 2003, CJTF–7 signed the theater's first policy on interrogation, which contained elements of the approved Guantanamo policy and elements of the Special Operations Forces policy. Policies approved for use on Al-Qaeda and Taliban detainees, who were not afforded the protection of the Geneva Conventions, now applied to detainees who did fall under the Geneva Convention protections.

Central Command disapproved the September 14, 2003, policy, resulting in another policy signed on October 12, 2003, which essentially mirrored the outdated 1987 version of the Field Manual 34–52. The 1987 version, however, authorized interrogators to control all aspects of the interrogation, "to include lighting and heating, as well as food, clothing, and shelter given to detainees." This was specifically left out of the current 1992 version. This clearly led to confusion on what practices were acceptable. We cannot be sure how much the number and severity of abuses would have been curtailed had there been early and consistent guidance from higher levels. Nonetheless, such guidance was needed and likely would have had a limiting effect.

At the tactical level we concur with the conclusion of

the investigation [by Lt. Gen. Anthony Jones and Maj. Gen. George Fay] that military intelligence personnel share responsibility for the abuses at Abu Ghraib with the military police soldiers cited in the investigation by [Maj. Gen. Antonio] Taguba. The Jones/Fay Investigation found 44 alleged instances of abuse, some which were also considered by the Taguba report. A number of these cases involved MI personnel directing the actions of MP personnel. Yet it should be noted that of the 66 closed cases of detainee abuse in Guantanamo, Afghanistan and Iraq cited by the Naval Inspector General, only one-third were interrogation related.

The Panel concurs with the findings of the Taguba and Jones investigations that serious leadership problems in the 800th MP Brigade and 205th MI Brigade, to include the 320th MP Battalion Commander and the Director of the Joint Debriefing and Interrogation Center, allowed the abuses at Abu Ghraib. The Panel endorses the disciplinary actions taken as a result of the Taguba Investigation. The Panel anticipates that the Chain of Command will take additional disciplinary action as a result of the referrals of the Jones/Fay investigation.

We believe Lieutenant General Sanchez should have taken stronger action in November when he realized the extent of the leadership problems at Abu Ghraib. His attempt to mentor Brig. Gen. [Janis] Karpinski, though well-intended, was insufficient in a combat zone in the midst of a serious and growing insurgency. Although Lieutenant General Sanchez had more urgent tasks than dealing personally with command and resource deficiencies at Abu Ghraib, Maj. Gen. [Walter] Wojdakowski and the staff should have seen that urgent demands were placed to higher headquarters for additional assets. We concur with the Jones findings that Lieutenant General Sanchez and Major General Wojdakowski failed to ensure proper staff oversight of detention and interrogation operations.

We note, however, in terms of its responsibilities, CJTF–7 was never fully resourced to meet the size and complexity of its mission. The Joint Staff, CJTF–7 and Central Command took too long to finalize the Joint Manning Document. It was not finally approved until December 2003, six months into the insurgency. At one point, CJTF–7 had only 495 of the 1,400 personnel authorized. The command was burdened with additional complexities associated with its mission to support the Coalition Provisional Authority.

Once it became clear in the summer of 2003 that there was a major insurgency growing in Iraq, with the potential for capturing a large number of enemy combatants, senior leaders should have moved to meet the need for additional military police forces. Certainly by October and November, when the fighting reached a new peak, commanders and staff from CJTF–7 all the way to Central Command to the Joint Chiefs of Staff should have known about and reacted to the serious limitations of the battalion of the 800th Military Police Brigade at Abu Ghraib. Central Command and the Joint Chiefs of Staff should have at least considered adding forces to the detention/interrogation mission. It is the judgment of this panel that in the future, considering the sensitivity of this kind of mission, the Office of the Secretary of Defense should assure itself that serious limitations in detention/interrogation missions do not occur.

Several options were available to the Commander of Central Command and above, including reallocation of U.S. Army assets already in the theater, Operational Control of other Service Military Police units in theater, and mobilization and deployment of additional forces from the continental United States. There is no evidence that any of the responsible senior officers considered any of these options. What could and should have been done more promptly is evidenced by the fact that the detention/interrogation operation in Iraq is now directed by a Major General reporting directly to the Commander, Multi-National Forces Iraq. Increased units of Military Police, fully manned and more appropriately equipped, are performing the mission once assigned to a single under-strength, poorly trained, inadequately equipped and weakly-led brigade.

In addition to the already cited leadership problems in the 800th MP Brigade, there were a series of tangled command relationships. These ranged from an unclear military intelligence chain of command, to the Tactical Control relationship of the 800th with CJTF–7 which the Brigade Commander apparently did not adequately understand, and the confusing and unusual assignment of

MI and MP responsibilities at Abu Ghraib. The failure to react appropriately to the October 2003 report of the International Committee of the Red Cross, following its two visits to Abu Ghraib, is indicative of the weakness of the leadership at Abu Ghraib. These unsatisfactory relationships were present neither at Guantanamo nor in Afghanistan.

Department of Defense reform efforts are underway and the Panel commends these efforts. They are discussed in more detail in the body of this report. The Office of the Secretary of Defense, the Joint Chiefs of Staff and the Military Services are conducting comprehensive reviews on how military operations have changed since the end of the Cold War. The Military Services now recognize the problems and are studying force compositions, training, doctrine, responsibilities and active duty/reserve and guard/contractor mixes which must be adjusted to ensure we are better prepared to succeed in the war on terrorism. As an example, the Army is currently planning and developing 27 additional MP companies.

The vast majority of detainees in Guantanamo, Afghanistan and Iraq were treated appropriately, and the great bulk of detention operations were conducted in compliance with U.S. policy and directives. They yielded significant amounts of actionable intelligence for dealing with the insurgency in Iraq and strategic intelligence of value in the Global War on Terror. For example, much of the information in the recently released 9/11 Commission's report, on the planning and execution of the attacks on the World Trade Center and Pentagon, came from interrogation of detainees at Guantanamo and elsewhere.

Justice Sandra Day O'Connor, writing for the majority of the Supreme Court of the United States in *Hamdi v. Rumsfeld* on June 28, 2004, pointed out that "The purpose of detention is to prevent captured individuals from returning to the field of battle and taking up arms once again." But detention operations also serve the key purpose of intelligence gathering. These are not competing interests but appropriate objectives which the United States may lawfully pursue.

We should emphasize that tens of thousands of men and women in uniform strive every day under austere and dangerous conditions to secure our freedom and the freedom of others. By historical standards, they rate as some of the best trained, disciplined and professional service men and women in our nation's history.

INTRODUCTION:
CHARTER AND METHODOLOGY

The Secretary of Defense chartered the Independent Panel on May 12, 2004, to review Department of Defense Detention Operations.... The Secretary asked for the Panel's independent advice in highlighting the issues considered most important for his attention. He asked for the Panel's views on the causes and contributing factors to problems in detainee operations and what corrective measures would be required....

The Panel did not conduct a case-by-case review of individual abuse cases. This task has been accomplished by those professionals conducting criminal and commander-directed investigations. Many of these investigations are still ongoing. The Panel did review the various completed and ongoing reports covering the causes for the abuse. Each of these inquiries or inspections defined abuse, categorized the abuses, and analyzed the abuses in conformity with the appointing authorities' guidance, but the methodologies do not parallel each other in all respects. The Panel concludes, based on our review of other reports to date and our own efforts, that causes for abuse have been adequately examined. . . .

THE CHANGING THREAT

The date September 11, 2001, marked an historic juncture in America's collective sense of security. On that day our presumption of invulnerability was irretrievably shattered. Over the last decade, the military has been called upon to establish and maintain the peace in Bosnia and Kosovo, eject the Taliban from Afghanistan, defeat the Iraqi Army, and fight ongoing insurgencies in Iraq and Afghanistan. Elsewhere it has been called upon to confront geographically dispersed terrorists who would threaten America's right to political sovereignty and our right to live free of fear.

In waging the Global War on Terror, the military confronts a far wider range of threats. In Iraq and Afghanistan,

U.S. forces are fighting diverse enemies with varying ideologies, goals and capabilities. American soldiers and their coalition partners have defeated the armored divisions of the Republican Guard, but are still under attack by forces using automatic rifles, rocket-propelled grenades, roadside bombs and surface-to-air missiles. We are not simply fighting the remnants of dying regimes or opponents of the local governments and coalition forces assisting those governments, but multiple enemies including indigenous and international terrorists. This complex operational environment requires soldiers capable of conducting traditional stability operations associated with peacekeeping tasks one moment and fighting force-on-force engagements normally associated with war-fighting the next moment.

Warfare under the conditions described inevitably generates detainees—enemy combatants, opportunists, trouble-makers, saboteurs, common criminals, former regime officials and some innocents as well. These people must be carefully but humanely processed to sort out those who remain dangerous or possess militarily-valuable intelligence. Such processing presents extraordinarily formidable logistical, administrative, security and legal problems completely apart from the technical obstacles posed by communicating with prisoners in another language and extracting actionable intelligence from them in a timely fashion. These activities, called detention operations, are a vital part of an expeditionary army's responsibility, but they depend upon training, skills and attributes not normally associated with soldiers in combat units.

Military interrogators and military police, assisted by front-line tactical units, found themselves engaged in detention operations with detention procedures still steeped in the methods of World War II and the Cold War, when those we expected to capture on the battlefield were generally a homogenous group of enemy soldiers. Yet this is a new form of war, not at all like Desert Storm nor even analogous to Vietnam or Korea. General [John] Abizaid [Commander, U.S. Central Command] himself best articulated the current nature of combat in testimony before the U.S. Senate Armed Services Committee on May 19, 2004:

> Our enemies are in a unique position, and they are a unique brand of ideological extremists whose vision of the world is best summed up by how the Taliban ran Afghanistan. If they can outlast us in Afghanistan and undermine the legitimate government there, they'll once again fill up the seats at the soccer stadium and force people to watch executions. If, in Iraq, the culture of intimidation practiced by our enemies is allowed to win, the mass graves will fill again. Our enemies kill without remorse, they challenge our will through the careful manipulation of propaganda and information, they seek safe havens in order to develop weapons of mass destruction that they will use against us when they are ready. Their targets are not Kabul

and Baghdad, but places like Madrid and London and New York. While we can't be defeated militarily, we're not going to win this thing militarily alone. ... As we fight this most unconventional war of this new century, we must be patient and courageous.

In Iraq the U.S. commanders were slow to recognize and adapt to the insurgency that erupted in the summer and fall of 2003. Military police and interrogators who had previous experience in the Balkans, Guantanamo and Afghanistan found themselves, along with increasing numbers of less-experienced troops, in the midst of detention operations in Iraq the likes of which the Department of Defense had not foreseen. As Combined Joint Task Force 7 began detaining thousands of Iraqis suspected of involvement in or having knowledge of the insurgency, the problem quickly surpassed the capacity of the staff to deal with and the wherewithal to contain it.

Line units conducting raids found themselves seizing specifically targeted persons, so designated by military intelligence; but, lacking interrogators and interpreters to make precise distinctions in an alien culture and hostile neighborhoods, they reverted to rounding up any and all suspicious-looking persons—all too often including women and children. The flood of incoming detainees contrasted sharply with the trickle of released individuals. Processing was overwhelmed. Some detainees at Abu Ghraib had been held 90 days before being interrogated for the first time.

Many interrogators, already in short supply from major reductions during the post-Cold War drawdown, by this time were on their second or third combat tour. Unit cohesion and morale were largely absent as under-strength companies and battalions from across the United States and Germany were deployed piecemeal and stitched together in a losing race to keep up with the rapid influx of vast numbers of detainees.

As the insurgency reached an initial peak in the fall of 2003, many military policemen from the Reserves who had been activated shortly after September 11, 2001, had reached the mandatory two-year limit on their mobilization time. Consequently, the ranks of soldiers having custody of detainees in Iraq fell to about half strength as MPs were ordered home by higher headquarters.

Some individuals seized the opportunity provided by this environment to give vent to latent sadistic urges. Moreover, many well-intentioned professionals, attempting to resolve the inherent moral conflict between using harsh techniques to gain information to save lives and treating detainees humanely, found themselves on uncharted ethical ground, with frequently changing guidance from above. Some stepped over the line of humane treatment accidentally; some did so knowingly. Some of the abusers believed other governmental agencies were conducting interrogations using harsher techniques than allowed by the Army Field Manual 34–52, a perception leading to the belief that such methods were condoned. In nearly 10 percent of the cases of alleged abuse, the chain of command ignored reports of those allegations. More than once a commander was complicit.

The requirements for successful detainee operations following major combat operations were known by U.S. forces in Iraq. After operations Enduring Freedom and earlier phases of Iraqi Freedom, several lessons learned were captured in official reviews and were available online to any authorized military user. These lessons included the need for doctrine tailored to enable police and interrogators to work together effectively; the need for keeping NO and MI units manned at levels sufficient to the task; and the need for MP and MI units to belong to the same tactical command. However, there is no evidence that those responsible for planning and executing detainee operations, in the phase of the Iraq campaign following the major combat operations, availed themselves of these "lessons learned" in a timely fashion.

Judged in a broader context, U.S. detention operations were both traditional and new. They were traditional in that detainee operations were a part of all past conflicts. They were new in that the Global War on Terror and the insurgency we are facing in Iraq present a much more complicated detainee population.

Many of America's enemies, including those in Iraq and Afghanistan, have the ability to conduct this new kind of warfare, often referred to as "asymmetric" warfare. Asymmetric warfare can be viewed as attempts to circumvent or undermine a superior, conventional strength, while exploiting its weaknesses using methods the superior force neither can defeat nor resort to itself. Small unconventional forces can violate a state's security without any state support or affiliation whatsoever. For this reason, many terms in the orthodox lexicon of war— e.g., state sovereignty, national borders, uniformed combatants, declarations of war, and even war itself—are not terms terrorists acknowledge.

Today, the power to wage war can rest in the hands of a few dozen highly motivated people with cell phones and access to the Internet. Going beyond simply terrorizing individual civilians, certain insurgent and terrorist organizations represent a higher level of threat, characterized by an ability and willingness to violate the political sovereignty and territorial integrity of sovereign nations.

Essential to defeating terrorist and insurgent threats is the ability to locate cells, kill or detain key leaders, and interdict operational and financial networks. However, the smallness and wide dispersal of these enemy assets make it problematic to focus on signal and imagery intelligence as we did in the Cold War, Desert Storm, and the first phase of Operation Iraqi Freedom. The ability of terrorists and insurgents to blend into the civilian population further decreases their vulnerability to signal and imagery intelligence. Thus, information gained from human sources, whether by spying or interrogation, is essential in narrowing the field upon which other intelligence gathering resources may be applied. In sum, human intelligence is absolutely necessary, not just to fill these gaps in information derived from other sources, but also to provide clues and leads for the other sources to exploit.

Military police functions must also adapt to this new kind of warfare. In addition to organizing more units capable of handling theater-level detention operations, we must also organize those units so they are able to deal with the heightened threat environment. In this new form of warfare, the distinction between front and rear becomes more fluid. All forces must continuously prepare for combat operations.

THE POLICY PROMULGATION PROCESS

Although there were a number of contributing causes for detainee abuses, policy processes were inadequate or deficient in certain respects at various levels: Department of Defense, Central Command, Coalition Forces Land Component Command, CJTF–7, and the individual holding facility or prison. In pursuing the question of the extent to which policy processes at the Department of Defense or national level contributed to abuses, it is important to begin with policy development as individuals in Afghanistan were first being detained in November 2001. The first detainees arrived at Guantanamo in January 2002.

In early 2002, a debate was ongoing in Washington on the application of treaties and laws to Al-Qaeda and the Taliban. The Department of Justice, Office of Legal

Counsel, advised Department of Defense General Counsel and the Counsel to the President that, among other things:

- Neither the Federal War Crimes Act nor the Geneva Conventions would apply to the detention conditions of Al-Qaeda prisoners.
- The President had the authority to suspend the United States treaty obligations applying to Afghanistan for the duration of the conflict should he determine Afghanistan to be a failed state.
- The President could find that the Taliban did not qualify for Enemy Prisoner of War status under Geneva Convention III.

The Attorney General and the Counsel to the President, in part relying on the opinions of Office of Legal Counsel, advised the President to determine the Geneva Conventions did not apply to the conflict with Al-Qaeda and the Taliban. The Panel understands Department of Defense General Counsel's position was consistent with the Attorney General's and the Counsel to the President's position. Earlier, the Department of State had argued that the Geneva Conventions in their traditional application provided a sufficiently robust legal construct under which the Global War on Terror could effectively be waged.

The Legal Advisor to the Chairman, Joint Chiefs of Staff, and many service lawyers agreed with the State Department's initial position. They were concerned that to conclude otherwise would be inconsistent with past practice and policy, jeopardize the United States armed forces personnel, and undermine the United States military culture which is based on a strict adherence to the law of war. At the February 4, 2002, National Security Council meeting to decide this issue, the Department of State, the Department of Defense, and the Chairman of the Joint Chiefs of Staff were in agreement that all detainees would get the treatment they are (or would be) entitled to under the Geneva Conventions.

On February 7, 2002, the President issued his decision memorandum. The memorandum stated the Geneva Conventions did not apply to Al-Qaeda and therefore they were not entitled to prisoner of war status. It also stated the Geneva Conventions did apply to the Taliban but the Taliban combatants were not entitled to prisoner of war status as a result of their failure to conduct themselves in accordance with the provisions of the Geneva Conventions. The President's memorandum also stated: "As a matter of policy, United States Armed Forces shall continue to treat detainees humanely and, to the extent appropriate and consistent with military necessity, in a manner consistent with the principles of Geneva."

Regarding the applicability of the Convention Against Torture and Other Cruel Inhumane or Degrading Treatment, the Office of Legal Counsel opined on August 1, 2002, that interrogation methods that comply with the relevant domestic law do not violate the Convention. It held that only the most extreme acts, that were specifically intended to inflict severe pain and torture, would be in violation; lesser acts might be "cruel, inhumane, or degrading," but would not violate the Convention Against Torture or domestic statutes. The Office of Legal Counsel memorandum went on to say, as Commander in Chief exercising his wartime powers, the President could even authorize torture, if he so decided.

Reacting to tenacious resistance by some detainees to existing interrogation methods, which were essentially limited to those in Army Field Manual 34–52, Guantanamo authorities in October 2002 requested approval of strengthened counter-interrogation techniques to increase the intelligence yield from interrogations. This request was accompanied by a recommended tiered list of techniques, with the proviso that the harsher Category III methods could be used only on "exceptionally resistant detainees" and with approval by higher headquarters.

This Guantanamo initiative resulted in a December 2, 2002 decision by the Secretary of Defense authorizing, "as a matter of policy," the use of Categories I and II and only one technique in Category III: mild, non-injurious physical contact. As a result of concern by the Navy General Counsel, the Secretary of Defense rescinded his December approval of all Category II techniques plus the one from Category III on January 15, 2003. This essentially returned interrogation techniques to Field Manual 34–52 guidance. He also stated if any of the methods from Categories II and III were deemed warranted, permission for their use should be requested from him.

The Secretary of Defense directed the Department of Defense General Counsel to establish a working group to study interrogation techniques. The working group was headed by Air Force General Counsel Mary Walker and included wide membership from across the military, legal and intelligence communities. The working group also relied heavily on the Office of Legal Counsel. The working group reviewed 35 techniques, and after a very expansive debate, ultimately recommended 24 to the Secretary of Defense. The study led to the Secretary's promulgation on April 16, 2003, of the list of approved techniques. His memorandum emphasized appropriate safeguards should be in place and, further, *"Use of these techniques is limited to interrogations of unlawful combatants held at Guantanamo Bay, Cuba."* He also stipulated that four of the techniques should be used only in case of military necessity and that he should be so notified in advance. If additional techniques were deemed essential, they should be requested in writing, with "recommended safeguards and rationale for applying with an identified detainee."

In the initial development of these Secretary of Defense policies, the legal resources of the Services' Judge Advocates and General Counsels were not utilized to their fullest potential. Had the Secretary of Defense had the benefit of a wider range of legal opinions and a more robust debate regarding detainee policies and operations, his policy of April 16, 2003, might well have been developed and issued in early December 2002. This could have avoided the policy changes which characterized the December 2, 2002, to April 16, 2003, period.

It is clear that pressure for additional intelligence and the more aggressive methods sanctioned by the Secretary of Defense memorandum resulted in stronger interrogation techniques. They did contribute to a belief that stronger interrogation methods were needed and appropriate in the treatment of detainees. At Guantanamo, the interrogators used those additional techniques with only two detainees, gaining important and time-urgent information in the process.

In Afghanistan, from the war's inception through the end of 2002, all forces used Field Manual 34–52 as a baseline for interrogation techniques. Nonetheless, more aggressive interrogation of detainees appears to have been ongoing. On January 24, 2003, in response to a data call from the Joint Staff to facilitate the Secretary of Defense—directed Working Group efforts, the Commander Joint Task Force 180 forwarded a list of techniques being used in Afghanistan, including some not explicitly set out in Field Manual 34–52. These techniques were included in a Special Operations Forces Standard Operating Procedures document published in February 2003. The 519th Military Intelligence Battalion, a Company of which was later sent to Iraq, assisted in interrogations in support of Special Operations Forces and was fully aware of their interrogation techniques.

In Iraq, the operational order from Central Command provided the standard Field Manual 34–52 interrogation procedures would be used. Given the greatly different situations in Afghanistan and Iraq, it is not surprising there were differing Central Command policies for the two countries. In light of ongoing hostilities that monopolized commanders' attention in Iraq, it is also not unexpected the detainee issues were not given a higher priority.

Interrogators and lists of techniques circulated from Guantanamo and Afghanistan to Iraq. During July and August 2003, a Company of the 519th MI Battalion was sent to the Abu Ghraib detention facility to conduct interrogation operations. Absent guidance other than Field Manual 34–52, the officer in charge prepared draft interrogation guidelines that were a near copy of the Standard Operating Procedure created by Special Operations Forces. It is important to note that techniques effective under carefully controlled conditions at Guantanamo became far more problematic when they migrated and were not adequately safeguarded.

In August 2003, Maj. Gen. Geoffrey Miller arrived to conduct an assessment of Department of Defense counterterrorism interrogation and detention operations in Iraq. He was to discuss current theater ability to exploit internees rapidly for actionable intelligence. He brought to Iraq the Secretary of Defense's April 16, 2003, policy guidelines for Guantanamo—which he reportedly gave to CJTF–7 as a potential model—recommending a command-wide policy be established. He noted, however, the Geneva Conventions did apply to Iraq. In addition to these various printed sources, there was also a store of common lore and practice within the interrogator community circulating through Guantanamo, Afghanistan and elsewhere.

At the operational level, in the absence of more specific guidance from Central Command, interrogators in Iraq relied on Field Manual 34–52 and on unauthorized techniques that had migrated from Afghanistan. On September 14, 2003, Commander CJTF–7 signed the theater's first policy on interrogation, which contained elements of the approved Guantanamo policy and elements of the Special Operations Forces policy. Policies approved for use on Al-Qaeda and Taliban detainees who were not afforded the protection of Enemy Prisoner of War status under the Geneva Conventions now applied to detainees who did fall under the Geneva Convention protections. Central Command disapproved the September 14, 2003, policy, resulting in another policy signed on October 12, 2003, which essentially mirrored the outdated 1987 version of the Field Manual 34–52. The 1987 version, however, authorized interrogators to control all aspects of the interrogation, "to include lighting and heating, as well as food, clothing, and shelter given to detainees." This was specifically left out of the 1992 version, which is currently in use. This clearly led to confusion on what practices were acceptable. We cannot be sure how much the number and severity of abuses would have been curtailed had there been early and consistent guidance from higher levels. Nonetheless, such guidance was needed and likely would have had a limiting effect.

At Abu Ghraib, the Jones/Fay investigation concluded that MI professionals at the prison level shared a "major part of the culpability" for the abuses. Some of the abuses occurred during interrogation. As these interrogation techniques exceeded parameters of Field Manual 34–52, no training had been developed. Absent training, the interrogators used their own initiative to implement the new techniques. To what extent the same situation existed at other prisons is unclear, but the widespread nature of abuses warrants an assumption that at least the understanding of interrogation policies was inadequate. A host of other possible contributing factors, such as training, leadership and the generally chaotic situation in the prisons, are addressed elsewhere in this report.

PUBLIC RELEASE OF ABUSE PHOTOS

In any large bureaucracy, good news travels up the chain of command quickly; bad news generally does not. In the case of the abuse photos from Abu Ghraib, concerns about command influence on an ongoing investigation may have impeded notification to senior officials.

Chronology of Events

On January 13, 2004, Specialist Darby gave Army criminal investigators a copy of a CD containing abuse photos he had taken from Specialist Graner's computer. CJTF–7, Central Command, the Chairman of the Joint Chiefs of

Staff and the Secretary of Defense were all informed of the issue. Lieutenant General Sanchez promptly asked for an outside investigation, and Major General Taguba was appointed as the investigating officer. The officials who saw the photos on January 14, 2004, not realizing their likely significance, did not recommend the photos be shown to more senior officials. A Central Command press release in Baghdad on January 16, 2004 announced there was an ongoing investigation into reported incidents of detainee abuse at a Coalition Forces detention facility.

An interim report of the investigation was provided to CJTF–7 and Central Command commanders in mid-March 2004. It is unclear whether they saw the Abu Ghraib photos, but their impact was not appreciated by either of these officers or their staff officers who may have seen the photographs, as indicated by the failure to transmit them in a timely fashion to more senior officials. When Lieutenant General Sanchez received the Taguba report, he immediately requested an investigation into the possible involvement of military intelligence personnel. He told the panel that he did not request the photos be disseminated beyond the criminal investigative process because commanders are prohibited from interfering with, or influencing, active investigations. In mid-April, Lt. Gen. [David] McKiernan, the appointing official, reported the investigative results through his chain of command to the Department of the Army, the Army Judge Advocate General, and the U.S. Army Reserve

Command. Lieutenant General McKiernan advised the panel that he did not send a copy of the report to the Secretary of Defense, but forwarded it through his chain of command. Again the reluctance to move bad news farther up the chain of command probably was a factor impeding notification of the Secretary of Defense.

Given this situation, Gen. Richard Myers, the Chairman of the Joint Chiefs of Staff, was unprepared in April 2004 when he learned the photos of detainee abuse were to be aired in a CBS broadcast. The planned release coincided with particularly intense fighting by Coalition forces in Fallujah and Najaf. After a discussion with General Abizaid, General Myers asked CBS to delay the broadcast out of concern the lives of the Coalition soldiers and the hostages in Iraq would be further endangered. The story of the abuse itself was already public. Nonetheless, both General Abizaid and General Myers understood the pictures would have an especially explosive impact around the world.

Informing Senior Officials

Given the magnitude of this problem, the Secretary of Defense and other senior Department of Defense officials need a more effective information pipeline to inform them of high-profile incidents which may have a significant adverse impact on Department of Defense operations. Had such a pipeline existed, it could have provided an accessible and efficient tool for field commanders to apprise higher headquarters, the Joint Chiefs of Staff, and the Office of the Secretary of Defense of actual or developing situations which might hinder, impede or undermine U.S. operations and initiatives. Such a system could have equipped senior spokesmen with the known facts of the situation from all Department of Defense elements involved. Finally, it would have allowed for senior official preparation and Congressional notification.

Such a procedure would make it possible for a field-level command or staff agency to alert others of the situation and forward the information to senior officials. This would not have been an unprecedented occurrence. For example, in December 2002, concerned Naval Criminal Investigative Service agents drew attention to the potential for abuse at Guantanamo. Those individuals had direct access to the highest levels of leadership and were able to get that information to senior levels without encumbrance. While a corresponding flow of information might not have prevented the abuses from occurring, the Office of the Secretary of Defense would have been alerted to a festering issue, allowing for an early and appropriate response.

Another example is the Air Force Executive Issues Team. This office has fulfilled the special information pipeline function for the Air Force since February 1998. The team chief and team members are highly trained and experienced field grade officers drawn from a variety of duty assignments. The team members have access to information flow across all levels of command and staff and are continually engaging and building contacts to facilitate the information flow. The information flow to the team runs parallel and complementary to standard reporting channels in order to avoid bypassing the chain of command, yet ensures a rapid and direct flow of relevant information to Air Force Headquarters.

A proper, transparent posture in getting the facts and fixing the problem would have better enabled the Department of Defense to deal with the damage to the mission of the U.S. in the region and to the reputation of the U.S. military.

COMMAND RESPONSIBILITIES

Although the most egregious instances of detainee abuse were caused by the aberrant behavior of a limited number of soldiers and the predilections of the non-commissioned officers on the night shift of Tier 1 at Abu Ghraib, the Independent Panel finds that commanding officers and their staffs at various levels failed in their duties and that such failures contributed directly or indirectly to detainee abuse. Commanders are responsible for all their units do or fail to do, and should be held accountable for their action or inaction. Command failures were compounded by poor advice provided by staff officers with responsibility for overseeing battlefield functions related to detention and interrogation operations. Military and civilian leaders at the Department of Defense share this burden of responsibility.

Commanders

The Panel finds that the weak and ineffectual leadership of the Commanding General of the 800th MP Brigade and the Commanding Officer of the 205th MI Brigade allowed the abuses at Abu Ghraib. There were serious lapses of leadership in both units from junior non-commissioned officers to battalion and brigade levels. The commanders of both brigades either knew, or should have known, abuses were taking place and taken measures to prevent them. The Panel finds no evidence that organizations above the 800th MP Brigade- or the 205th MI Brigade-level were directly involved in the incidents at Abu Ghraib. Accordingly, the Panel concurs in the judgment and recommendations of Major General Taguba, Major General Fay, Lieutenant General Jones, Lieutenant General Sanchez, Lieutenant General McKiernan, General Abizaid and General [Paul] Kern regarding the commanders of these two units. The Panel expects disciplinary action may be forthcoming.

The Independent Panel concurs with the findings of Major General Taguba regarding the Director of the Joint Interrogation and Debriefing Center at Abu Ghraib. Specifically, the Panel notes that Major General Taguba concluded that the Director, Joint Interrogation and Debriefing Center, made material misrepresentations to Major General Taguba's investigating team. The panel finds that he failed to properly train and control his soldiers and failed to ensure prisoners were afforded the protections under the relevant Geneva Conventions. The

Panel concurs with Major General Taguba's recommendation that he be relieved for cause and given a letter of reprimand and notes that disciplinary action may be pending against this officer.

The Independent Panel concurs with the findings of Major General Taguba regarding the Commander of the 320th MP Battalion at Abu Ghraib. Specifically, the Panel finds that he failed to ensure that his subordinates were properly trained and supervised and that he failed to establish and enforce basic soldier standards, proficiency and accountability. He was not able to organize tasks to accomplish his mission in an appropriate manner. By not communicating standards, policies and plans to soldiers, he conveyed a sense of tacit approval of abusive behavior toward prisoners and a lax and dysfunctional command climate took hold. The Panel concurs with Major General Taguba's recommendation that he be relieved of command, be given a General Officer Memorandum of reprimand, and be removed from the Colonel/O–6 promotion list.

The Independent Panel finds that Brigadier General Karpinski's leadership failures helped set the conditions at the prison which led to the abuses, including her failure to establish appropriate standard operating procedures and to ensure the relevant Geneva Conventions protections were afforded prisoners, as well as her failure to take appropriate actions regarding ineffective commanders and staff officers. The Panel notes the conclusion of Major General Taguba that she made material misrepresentations to his investigating team regarding the frequency of her visits to Abu Ghraib. The Panel concurs with Major General Taguba's recommendation that Brigadier General Karpinski be relieved of command and given a General Officer Letter of Reprimand.

Although Lieutenant General Sanchez had tasks more urgent than dealing personally with command and resource deficiencies and allegations of abuse at Abu Ghraib, he should have ensured his staff dealt with the command and resource problems. He should have assured that urgent demands were placed for appropriate support and resources through Coalition Forces Land Component Command and Central Command to the Joint Chiefs of Staff. He was responsible for establishing the confused command relationship at the Abu Ghraib prison. There was no clear delineation of command responsibilities between the 320th MP Battalion and the 205th MI Brigade. The situation was exacerbated by CJTF–7 Fragmentary Order 1108 issued on November 19, 2003, that appointed the commander of the 205th MI Brigade as the base commander for Abu Ghraib, including responsibility for the support of all MPs assigned to the prison. In addition to being contrary to existing doctrine, there is no evidence the details of this command relationship were effectively coordinated or implemented by the leaders at Abu Ghraib. The unclear chain of command established by CJTF–7, combined with the poor leadership and lack of supervision, contributed to the atmosphere at Abu Ghraib that allowed the abuses to take place.

The unclear command structure at Abu Ghraib was

further exacerbated by the confused command relationship up the chain. The 800th MP Brigade was initially
assigned to the Central Command's Combined Forces
Land Component Commander during the major combat
phase of Operation Iraqi Freedom. When [that com-
mander] left the theater and returned to Fort McPherson,
Georgia, Central Command established Combined Joint
Task Force 7. While the 800th MP Brigade remained
assigned to Combined Forces Land Component Command, it essentially worked for CJTF–7. Lieutenant General Sanchez delegated responsibility for detention
operations to his Deputy, Major General Wojdakowski.
At the same time, intelligence personnel at Abu Ghraib
reported through the CJTF–7 C–2, Director for Intelligence. These arrangements had the damaging result that
no single individual was responsible for overseeing operations at the prison.

The Panel endorses the disciplinary actions already
taken, although we believe Lieutenant General Sanchez
should have taken more forceful action in November
when he fully comprehended the depth of the leadership
problems at Abu Ghraib. His apparent attempt to mentor
Brigadier General Karpinski, though well-intended, was
insufficient in a combat zone in the midst of a serious and
growing insurgency.

The creation of the Joint Interrogation and Debriefing
Center at Abu Ghraib was not an unusual organizational
approach. The problem is, as the Army Inspector General
assessment revealed, joint doctrine for the conduct of

interrogation operations contains inconsistent guidance, particularly with regard to addressing the issue of the appropriate command relationships governing the operation of such organizations as a Joint Interrogation and Debriefing Center. Based on the investigative findings of Fay, Jones and [Vice Adm. Albert] Church [Naval Inspector General], Southern Command and Central Command were able to develop effective command relationships for such centers at Guantanamo and in Afghanistan, but Central Command and CJTF–7 failed to do so for the Joint Interrogation and Debriefing Center at Abu Ghraib.

Staff Officers

While staff officers have no command responsibilities, they are responsible for providing oversight, advice and counsel to their commanders. Staff oversight of detention and interrogation operations for CJTF–7 was dispersed among the principal and special staff. The lack of one person on the staff to oversee detention operations and facilities complicated effective and efficient coordination among the staff. The Panel finds the following:

- The CJTF–7 Deputy Commander failed to initiate action to request additional military police for detention operations after it became clear that there were insufficient assets in Iraq.
- The CJTF–7 C–2, Director for Intelligence, failed to advise the commander properly on directives and

policies needed for the operation of the Joint Interrogation and Debriefing Center, for interrogation
techniques and for appropriately monitoring the
activities of other government agencies within the
Joint Area of Operations.

■ The CJTF–7 Staff Judge Advocate failed to initiate
an appropriate response to the November 2003
International Committee of the Red Cross report
on the conditions at Abu Ghraib.

Failure of the Combatant Command to Adjust the Plan

Once it became clear in July 2003 that there was a major
insurgency growing in Iraq and the relatively benign environment projected for Iraq was not materializing, senior
leaders should have adjusted the plan from what had been
assumed to be a stability operation and a benign handoff
of detention operations to the Iraqis. If commanders and
staffs at the operational level had been more adaptive in
the face of changing conditions, a different approach to
detention operations could have been developed by October 2003, as difficulties with the basic plan were readily
apparent by that time. Responsible leaders who could
have set in motion the development of a more effective
alternative course of action extend up the command chain
(and staff), to include the Director for Operations, Combined Joint Task Force 7; Deputy Commanding General,
CJTF–7; Commander CJTF–7; Deputy Commander for
Support, Combined Forces Land Component Command;

Commander, Combined Forces Land Component Command; Director for Operations, Central Command; Commander, Central Command; Director for Operations, Joint Staff; the Chairman of the Joint Chiefs of Staff; and the Office of the Secretary of Defense. In most cases these were errors of omission, but they were errors that should not go unnoted.

There was ample evidence in both Joint and Army lessons learned that planning for detention operations for Iraq required alternatives to standard doctrinal approaches. Reports from experiences in Operation Enduring Freedom and at Guantanamo had already recognized the inadequacy of current doctrine for the detention mission and the need for augmentation of both MP and MI units with experienced confinement officers and interrogators. Previous experience also supported the likelihood that detainee population numbers would grow beyond planning estimates. The relationship between MP and MI personnel in the conduct of interrogations also demanded close, continuous coordination rather than remaining compartmentalized. "Lessons learned" also reported the value of establishing a clear chain of command subordinating MP and MI to a Joint Task Force or Brigade Commander. This commander would be in charge of all aspects of both detention and interrogations, just as tactical combat forces are subordinated to a single commander. The planners had only to search the lessons learned databases (available on-line in military networks) to find these planning insights. Nevertheless,

Central Command's October 2002 planning annex for detention operations reflected a traditional doctrinal methodology.

The change in the character of the struggle signaled by the sudden spike in U.S. casualties in June, July and August 2003 should have prompted consideration of the need for additional MP assets. General Abizaid himself signaled a change in operations when he publicly declared in July that Central Command was now dealing with a growing "insurgency," a term government officials had previously avoided in characterizing the war. Certainly by October and November, when the fighting reached a new peak, commanders and staffs from CJTF–7 all the way to Central Command and the Joint Chiefs of Staff knew the serious deficiencies of the 800th MP Brigade and should have at least considered reinforcing the troops for detention operations. Reservists, some of whom had been first mobilized shortly after September 11, 2001, began reaching a two-year mobilization commitment, which, by law, mandated their redeployment and deactivation.

There was not much the 800th MP Brigade (an Army Reserve unit) could do to delay the loss of those soldiers, and there was no individual replacement system or a unit replacement plan. The MP Brigade was totally dependent on higher headquarters to initiate action to alleviate the personnel crisis. The brigade was duly reporting readiness shortfalls through appropriate channels. However, its commanding general was emphasizing these shortfalls

in personal communications with CJTF–7 commanders
and staff as opposed to Combined Forces Land Component Command. Since the brigade was assigned to Combined Forces Land Component Command, but under the
Tactical Control of CJTF–7, her communications should
have been with Combined Forces Land Component
Command. The response from CJTF–7's Commander
and Deputy Commander was that the 800th MP Brigade
had sufficient personnel to accomplish its mission and
that it needed to reallocate its available soldiers among
the dozen or more detention facilities it was operating in
Iraq. However, the Panel found the further deterioration
in the readiness condition of the brigade should have
been recognized by Combined Forces Land Component
Command and Central Command by late summer 2003.
This led the Panel to conclude that CJTF–7, Combined
Forces Land Component Command and Central Command failure to request additional forces was an avoid-
able error.

The Joint Staff recognized intelligence collection from
detainees in Iraq needed improvement. This was their
rationale for sending Major General Miller from Guantanamo to assist CJTF–7 with interrogation operations.
However, the Joint Staff was not paying sufficient attention to evidence of broader readiness issues associated
with both MP and MI resources.

We note that CJTF–7 Headquarters was never fully
resourced to meet the size and complexity of its mission.
The Joint Staff, CJTF–7 and Central Command took too

long to finalize the Joint Manning Document, which was not finally approved until December 2003—six months into the insurgency. At one point, CJTF–7 Headquarters had only 495 of the 1,400 personnel authorized. The command was burdened with additional complexities associated with its mission to support the Coalition Provisional Authority.

Finally, the Joint Staff failed to recognize the implications of the deteriorating manning levels in the 800th MP Brigade; the absence of combat equipment among detention elements of MP units operating in a combat zone; and the indications of deteriorating mission performance among military intelligence interrogators owing to the stress of repeated combat deployments.

When CJTF–7 did realize the magnitude of the detention problem, it requested an assistance visit by the Provost Marshal General of the Army, Maj. Gen. [Donald] Ryder. There seemed to be some misunderstanding of the CJTF–7 intent, however, since Major General Ryder viewed his visit primarily as an assessment of how to transfer the detention program to the Iraqi prison system.

In retrospect, several options for addressing the detention operations challenge were available. CJTF–7 could have requested a change in command relationships to place the 800th MP Brigade under Operational Control of CJTF–7 rather than Tactical Control. This would have permitted the Commander of CJTF–7 to reallocate tactical assets under his control to the detention mission. While other Military Police units in Iraq were already fully committed to higher-priority combat and combat support missions, such as convoy escort, there were non-MP units that could have been reassigned to help in the conduct of detention operations. For example, an artillery brigade was tasked to operate the CJTF–7 Joint Visitors Center in Baghdad. A similar tasking could have provided additional troop strength to assist the 800th MP Brigade at Abu Ghraib. Such a shift would have supplied valuable experienced sergeants, captains and lieutenant colonels sorely lacking in both the MI and MP units at Abu Ghraib. A similar effect could have been achieved by Central Command assigning U.S. Marine Corps, Navy and Air Force MP and security units to operational control of CJTF–7 for the detention operations mission.

Mobilization and deployment of additional forces from the United States was also a feasible option. A system is in place for commands such as CJTF–7, Combined Forces Land Component Command and Central Command to submit a formal Request for Forces. Earlier, CJTF–7 had submitted [such a request] for an additional Judge Advocate organization, but Central Command would not forward it to the Joint Chiefs of Staff. Perhaps this experience made CJTF–7 reluctant to submit a [request] for MP units, but there is no evidence that any of the responsible officers considered any option other than the response given to Brigadier General Karpinski, to "wear her stars" and reallocate personnel among her already over-stretched units.

While it is the responsibility of the Joint Chiefs of Staff and services to provide adequate numbers of appropriately trained personnel for missions such as the detention operations in Iraq, it is the responsibility of the combatant commander to organize those forces in a manner to achieve mission success. The U.S. experience in the conduct of post-conflict stability operations has been limited, but the impact of our failure to conduct proper detainee operations in this case has been significant. Combatant commanders and their subordinates must organize in a manner that affords unity of command, ensuring commanders work for commanders and not staff.

The fact that the detention operation mission for all of Iraq is now commanded by a two-star general who reports directly to the operational commander, and that 1,900 MPs, more appropriately equipped for combat, now perform the mission once assigned to a single under-strength, poorly trained, inadequately equipped, and weakly-led brigade, indicate more robust options should have been considered sooner.

Finally, the panel notes the failure to report the abuses up the chain of command in a timely manner with adequate urgency. The abuses at Abu Ghraib were known and under investigation as early as January 2004. However, the gravity of the abuses was not conveyed up the chain of command to the Secretary of Defense. The Taguba report, including the photographs, was completed in March 2004. This report was transmitted to

Lieutenant General Sanchez and General Abizaid; however, it is unclear whether they ever saw the Abu Ghraib photos. General Myers has stated he knew of the existence of the photos as early as January 2004. Although the knowledge of the investigation into Abu Ghraib was widely known, as we noted in the previous section, the impact of the photos was not appreciated by any of these officers as indicated by the failure to transmit them in a timely fashion to officials at the Department of Defense.

MILITARY POLICE AND DETENTION OPERATIONS

In Operation Enduring Freedom in Afghanistan and Operation Iraqi Freedom, commanders should have paid greater attention to the relationship between detainees and military operations. The current doctrine and procedures for detaining personnel are inadequate to meet the requirements of these conflicts. Due to the vastly different circumstances in these conflicts, it should not be surprising there were deficiencies in the projected needs for military police forces. All the investigations the Panel reviewed highlight the urgency to augment the prior way of conducting detention operations. In particular, the military police were not trained, organized, or equipped to meet the new challenges.

The Army Inspector General found morale was high and command climate was good throughout forces deployed in Iraq and Afghanistan with one noticeable exception. Soldiers conducting detainee operations in remote or dangerous locations complained of very poor morale and command climate due to the lack of higher command involvement and support and the perception that their leaders did not care. At Abu Ghraib, in particular, there were many serious problems, which could have been avoided if proper guidance, oversight and leadership had been provided.

Mobilization and Training

Mobilization and training inadequacies for the MP units occurred during the various phases of employment, beginning with peacetime training, activation, arrival at the mobilization site, deployment, arrival in theater and follow-on operations.

Mobilization and Deployment

Problems generally began for the MP units upon arrival at the mobilization sites. As one commander stated, "Anything that could go wrong went wrong." Preparation was not consistently applied to all deploying units, wasting time and duplicating efforts already accomplished. Troops were separated from their equipment for excessive periods of time. The flow of equipment and personnel was not coordinated. The Commanding General of the 800th MP Brigade indicated the biggest problem was getting MPs and their equipment deployed together. The unit could neither train at its stateside mobilization site without its equipment nor upon arrival overseas, as two or three weeks could go by before joining with its equipment. This resulted in assigning equipment and troops in an *ad hoc* manner with no regard to original unit. It also resulted in assigning certain companies that had not trained together in peacetime to battalion headquarters. The flow of forces into theater was originally planned and assigned on the basis of the Time Phased Force Deployment List. The [list] was soon scrapped, however, in favor of individual unit deployment orders assigned by U.S. Army Forces Command based on unit readiness and personnel strength. MP Brigade commanders did not know who would be deployed next. This method resulted in a condition wherein a recently arrived battalion headquarters would be assigned the next arriving MP companies, regardless of their capabilities or any other prior command and training relationships.

Original projections called for approximately 12 detention facilities with a projection of 30,000 to 100,000 enemy prisoners of war. These large projections did not materialize. In fact, the initial commanding general of the 800th MP brigade, Brigadier General Hill, stated he had more than enough MPs designated for the Internment/Resettlement (hereafter called detention) mission at the end of the combat phase in Iraq. This assessment radically changed following the major combat phase, when the 800th moved to Baghdad beginning in the summer of 2003 to assume the detention mission. The brigade was given additional tasks assisting the Coalition Provisional Authority in reconstructing the Iraqi corrections system, a mission they had neither planned for nor anticipated.

Inadequate Training for the Military Police Mission

Though some elements performed better than others, generally training was inadequate. The MP detention units did not receive detention-specific training during their mobilization period, which was a critical deficiency. Detention training was conducted for only two MP detention battalions, one in Afghanistan and elements of the other at Camp Arifjan, Kuwait. The 800th MP Brigade, prior to deployment, had planned for a major detention exercise during the summer of 2002; however, this was cancelled due to the activation of many individuals and units for Operation Noble Eagle following the September 11, 2001, attack. The Deputy Commander of one MP brigade stated that "training at the mobilization site was wholly inadequate." In addition, there was no theater-specific training.

The Army Inspector General's investigators also found that training at the mobilization sites failed to prepare units for conducting detention operations. Leaders of inspected reserve units stated in interviews that they did not receive a clear mission statement prior to mobilization and were not notified of their mission until after deploying. Personnel interviewed described being placed immediately in stressful situations in a detention facility with thousands of non-compliant detainees and not being trained to handle them. Units arriving in theater were given just a few days to conduct a handover from the outgoing units. Once deployed, these newly arrived units had difficulty gaining access to the necessary documentation on tactics, techniques, and procedures to train their personnel on the MP-essential tasks of their new mission. A prime example is that relevant Army manuals and publications were available only on-line, but personnel did not have access to computers or the Internet.

Force Structure Organization

The current military police organizational structure does not address the detention mission on the nonlinear battlefield characteristic of the Global War on Terror.

Current Military Police Structure

The present U.S. Army Reserve and Army National Guard system worked well for the 1991 Gulf War, for which large numbers of reserve forces were mobilized, were deployed, fought, and were quickly returned to the United States. These forces, however, were not designed to maintain large numbers of troops at a high operational tempo for a long period of deployment as has been the case in Afghanistan and Iraq.

Comments from commanders and the various inspection reports indicated the current force structure for the MPs is neither flexible enough to support the developing mission, nor can it provide for the sustained detainee operations envisioned for the future. The primary reason is that the present structure lacks sufficient numbers of detention specialists. Currently, the Army active component detention specialists are assigned in support of the Disciplinary Barracks and Regional Correctional Facilities in the United States, all of which are non-deployable.

New Force Structure Initiatives

Significant efforts are currently being made to shift more of the MP detention requirements into the active force structure. The Army's force design for the future will standardize detention forces between active and reserve components and provide the capability for the active component to immediately deploy detention companies.

The Panel notes that the [study by the Army Inspector General, Lt. Gen. Paul] Mikolashek, found significant shortfalls in training and force structure for field sanitation, preventive medicine and medical treatment requirements for detainees.

Doctrine and Planning

Initial planning envisaged a conflict mirroring operation Desert Storm; approximately 100,000 enemy prisoners of war were forecast for the first five days of the conflict. This expectation did not materialize in the first phase of Operation Iraqi Freedom. As a result, there were too many MP detention companies. The reverse occurred in the second phase of Iraqi Freedom, where the plan envisaged a reduced number of detention MPs on the assumption the initial large numbers of enemy prisoners of war would already have been processed out of the detention facilities. The result was that combat MPs were ultimately reassigned to an unplanned detention mission.

The doctrine of yesterday's battlefield does not satisfy the requirements of today's conflicts. Current doctrine assumes a linear battlefield and is very clear for the handling of detainees from the point of capture to the holding areas and eventually to the detention facilities in the rear. However, Operations Enduring Freedom and Iraqi Freedom, both occurring where there is no distinction between front and rear areas, forced organizations to adapt tactics and procedures to address the resulting voids. Organizations initially used standard operating procedures for collection points and detention facilities. These procedures do not fit the new environment, generally because there are no safe areas behind "friendly lines"—there are no friendly lines. The inapplicability of current doctrine had a negative effect on accountability, security, safeguarding of detainees, and intelligence exploitation. Instead of capturing and rapidly moving detainees to secure collection points as prescribed by doctrine, units tended to retain the detainees and attempted to exploit their tactical intelligence value without the required training or infrastructure.

Current doctrine specifies that line combat units hold detainees no longer than 12–24 hours to extract immediately useful intelligence. Nonetheless, the Army Inspector General's inspection found detainees were routinely held up to 72 hours. For corps collection points, doctrine specifies detainees be held no longer than three days; the Army Inspector General found detainees were held from 30 to 45 days.

Equipment Shortfalls

The current force structure for MP detention organizations does not provide sufficient assets to meet the inherent force protection requirement on battlefields likely to be characteristic of the future. Detention facilities in the theater may have to be located in a hostile combat zone, instead of the benign secure environment current doctrine presumes.

MP detention units will need to be equipped for combat. Lack of crew-served weapons, e.g., machine guns and mortars, to counter external attacks resulted in casualties to the detainee population as well as to the friendly forces. Moreover, Army-issued radios were frequently inoperable and too few in number. In frustration, individual soldiers purchased commercial radios from civilian sources. This improvisation created an unsecured communications environment that could be monitored by any hostile force outside the detention facility.

Detention Operations and Accountability

Traditionally, military police support the Joint Task Force by undertaking administrative processing of detention operations, thereby relieving the war-fighters of concern over prisoners and civilian detainees. The handling of detainees is a tactical and operational consideration the Joint Task Force addresses during planning to prevent combat forces from being diverted to handle large numbers of detainees. Military police are structured, therefore, to facilitate the tempo of combat operations by providing for the quick movement of prisoners from the battle area to temporary holding areas and thence to detention facilities.

However, the lack of relevant doctrine meant the design and operation of division, battalion, and company collection points were improvised on an *ad hoc* basis, depending on such immediate local factors as mission, troops available, weather, time, etc. At these collection points, the standard operating procedures the units had prior to deployment were outdated or ill-suited for the operating environment of Afghanistan and Iraq. Tactical units found themselves taking on roles in detainee operations never anticipated in their prior training. Such lack of proper skills had a negative effect on the intelligence exploitation, security, and safeguarding of detainees.

The initial point of capture may be at any time or place in a military operation. This is the place where soldiers have the least control of the environment and where most contact with the detainees occurs. It is also the place where, in or immediately after battle, abuse may be most likely. And it is the place where the detainee, shocked by capture, may be most likely to give information. As noted earlier, instead of capturing and rapidly transporting detainees to collection points, battalions and companies were holding detainees for excessive periods, even though they lacked the training, materiel, or infrastructure for productive interrogation. The Naval Inspector General found that approximately one-third of the alleged incidents of abuse occurred at the point of capture.

Detention

The decision to use Abu Ghraib as the primary operational level detention facility happened by default. Abu Ghraib was selected by Ambassador [L. Paul] Bremer, who envisioned it as a temporary facility to be used for criminal detainees until the new Iraqi government could be established and an Iraqi prison established at another site. However, CJTF–7 saw an opportunity to use it as an interim site for the detainees it expected to round up as part of Operation Victory Bounty in July 2003. CJTF–7 had considered Camp Bucca but rejected it, as it was 150 miles away from Baghdad where the operation was to take place.

Abu Ghraib was also a questionable facility from a standpoint of conducting interrogations. Its location, next to an urban area, and its large size in relation to the small MP unit tasked to provide a law enforcement presence, made it impossible to achieve the necessary degree of security. The detainee population of approximately 7,000 out-manned the 92 MPs by approximately a 75:1 ratio. The choice of Abu Ghraib as the facility for detention operations placed a strictly detention mission-driven unit—one designed to operate in a rear area—smack in the middle of a combat environment.

Detainee Accountability and Classification

Adequate procedures for accountability were lacking during the movement of detainees from the collection points to the detainee facilities. During the movement, it was not unusual for detainees to exchange their identification tags with those of other detainees. The diversity of the detainee population also made identification and classification difficult. Classification determined the detainee assignment to particular cells/blocks, but individuals brought to the facility were often a mix of criminals and security detainees. The security detainees were either held for their intelligence value or presented a continuing threat to Coalition Forces. Some innocents were also included in the detainee population. The issue of unregistered or "ghost" detainees presented a limited, though significant problem of accountability at Abu Ghraib.

Detainee Reporting

Detainee reporting lacked accountability, reliability and standardization. There was no central agency to collect and manage detainee information. The combatant commanders and the Joint Task Force commanders have overall responsibility for the detainee programs to ensure compliance with the international law of armed conflict, domestic law and applicable national policy and directives. The reporting system is supposed to process all inquiries concerning detainees and provide accountability information to the International Committee of the Red Cross. The poor reporting system did not meet this obligation.

Release Procedures

Multiple reviews were required to make release recommendations prior to approval by the release authority. Nonconcurrence by area commanders, intelligence organizations, or law enforcement agencies resulted in retention of ever larger numbers of detainees. The Army Inspector General estimated that up to 80 percent of detainees being held for security and intelligence reasons might be eligible for release upon proper review of their cases, with the other 20 percent either requiring continued detention on security grounds or uncompleted intelligence requirements. Interviews indicated area commanders were reluctant to concur with release decisions out of concern that potential combatants would be reintroduced into their areas of operation or that the detainees had continuing intelligence value.

INTERROGATION OPERATIONS

Any discussion of interrogation techniques must begin with the simple reality that their purpose is to gain intelligence that will help protect the United States, its forces and interests abroad. The severity of the post-September 11, 2001, terrorist threat and the escalating insurgency in Iraq make information gleaned from interrogations especially important. When lives are at stake, all legal and moral means of eliciting information must be considered. Nonetheless, interrogations are inherently unpleasant, and many people find them objectionable by their very nature.

The relationship between interrogators and detainees is frequently adversarial. The interrogator's goal of extracting useful information likely is in direct opposition to the detainee's goal of resisting or dissembling. Although interrogators are trained to stay within the bounds of acceptable conduct, the imperative of eliciting timely and useful information can sometimes conflict with proscriptions against inhumane or degrading treatment. For interrogators in Iraq and Afghanistan, this tension is magnified by the highly stressful combat environment. The conditions of war and the dynamics of detainee operations carry inherent risks for human mistreatment and must be approached with caution and careful planning and training.

A number of interrelated factors both limited the intelligence derived from interrogations and contributed to detainee abuse in operations Enduring Freedom and Iraqi

Freedom. A shortfall of properly trained human intelligence personnel to do tactical interrogation of detainees existed at all levels. At the larger detention centers, qualified and experienced interrogators and interpreters were in short supply. No doctrine existed to cover segregation of detainees whose status differed or was unclear, nor was there guidance on timely release of detainees no longer deemed of intelligence interest. The failure to adapt rapidly to the new intelligence requirements of the Global War on Terror resulted in inadequate resourcing, inexperienced and untrained personnel, and a backlog of detainees destined for interrogation. These conditions created a climate not conducive to sound intelligence-gathering efforts.

The Threat Environment

The Global War on Terror requires a fundamental reexamination of how we approach collecting intelligence. Terrorists present new challenges because of the way they organize, communicate, and operate. Many of the terrorists and insurgents are geographically dispersed non-state actors who move across national boundaries and operate in small cells that are difficult to surveil and penetrate.

Human Intelligence from Interrogations

The need for human intelligence has dramatically increased in the new threat environment of asymmetric warfare. Massed forces and equipment characteristic of the Cold War era, Desert Storm and even Phase I of Operation Iraqi Freedom relied largely on signals and imagery intelligence. The intelligence problem then was primarily one of monitoring known military sites, troop locations and equipment concentrations. The problem today, however, is discovering new information on widely dispersed terrorist and insurgent networks. Human intelligence often provides the clues to understand these networks, enabling the collection of intelligence from other sources. Information derived from interrogations is an important component of this human intelligence, especially in the Global War on Terror.

The interrogation of Al-Qaeda members held at Guantanamo has yielded valuable information used to disrupt and preempt terrorist planning and activities. Much of the 9/11 Commission's report on the planning and execution of the attacks on the World Trade Center and Pentagon came from interrogation of detainees. In the case of Al-Qaeda, interrogations provided insights on organization, key personnel, target selection, planning cycles, cooperation among various groups, and logistical support. This information expanded our knowledge of the selection, motivation, and training of these groups. According to Congressional testimony by the Under Secretary of Defense for Intelligence, we have gleaned information on a wide range of Al-Qaeda activities, including efforts to obtain weapons of mass destruction, sources of finance, training in use of explosives and suicide bombings, and potential travel routes to the United States.

Interrogations provide commanders with information about enemy networks, leadership, and tactics. Such information is critical in planning operations. Tactically, detainee interrogation is a fundamental tool for gaining insight into enemy positions, strength, weapons, and intentions. Thus, it is fundamental to the protection of our forces in combat. Notably, Saddam Hussein's capture was facilitated by interrogation-derived information. Interrogations often provide fragmentary pieces of the broader intelligence picture. These pieces become useful when combined with other human intelligence or intelligence from other sources.

Pressure on Interrogators to Produce Actionable Intelligence

With the active insurgency in Iraq, pressure was placed on the interrogators to produce "actionable" intelligence. In the months before Saddam Hussein's capture, inability to determine his whereabouts created widespread frustration within the intelligence community. With lives at stake, senior leaders expressed, forcibly at times, their needs for better intelligence. A number of visits by high-level officials to Abu Ghraib undoubtedly contributed to this perceived pressure. Both the CJTF–7 commander and his intelligence officer, CJTF–7 C2, visited the prison on several occasions. Major General Miller's visit in August/September, 2003 stressed the need to move from simply collecting tactical information to collecting information of operational and strategic value. In November 2003, a senior member of the National Security Council Staff visited Abu Ghraib, leading some personnel at the facility to conclude, perhaps incorrectly, that even the White House was interested in the intelligence gleaned from their interrogation reports. Despite the number of visits and the intensity of interest in actionable intelligence, however, the Panel found no undue pressure exerted by senior officials. Nevertheless, their eagerness for intelligence may have been perceived by interrogators as pressure.

Interrogation Operations Issues

A number of factors contributed to the problems experienced in interrogation operations. They ranged from resource and leadership shortfalls to doctrinal deficiencies and poor training.

Inadequate Resources

As part of the peace dividend following the Cold War, much of the human intelligence capability, particularly in the Army, was reduced. As hostilities began in Afghanistan and Iraq, Army human intelligence personnel, particularly interrogators and interpreters, were ill-equipped to deal with requirements at both the tactical level and at the larger detention centers. At the tactical level, questioning of detainees has been used in all major conflicts.

Knowledge of the enemy's positions, strength, equipment and tactics is critical in order to achieve operational success while minimizing casualties. Such tactical questioning to gain immediate battlefield intelligence is generally done at or near the point of capture. In Iraq, although their numbers were insufficient, some of the more seasoned MIs from the MI units supporting Abu Ghraib were assigned to support the Army Tactical human intelligence teams in the field.

In both Afghanistan and Iraq, tactical commanders kept detainees longer than specified by doctrine in order to exploit their unique local knowledge, such as religious and tribal affiliation and regional politics. Remaining with the tactical units, the detainees could be available for follow-up questioning and clarification of details. The field commanders were concerned that information from interrogations, obtained in the more permanent facilities, would not be returned to the capturing unit. Tactical units, however, were not properly resourced to implement this altered operating arrangement. The potential for abuse also increases when interrogations are conducted in an emotionally charged field environment by personnel unfamiliar with approved techniques.

At the fixed detention centers such as Abu Ghraib, lack of resources and shortage of more experienced senior interrogators impeded the production of actionable intelligence. Inexperienced and untrained personnel often yielded poor intelligence. Interpreters, particularly, were in short supply, contributing to the backlog of detainees to be interrogated. As noted previously, at Abu Ghraib for instance, there were detainees who had been in custody for as long as 90 days before being interrogated for the first time.

Leadership and Organization Shortfalls at Abu Ghraib

Neither the leadership nor the organization of Military Intelligence at Abu Ghraib was up to the mission. The 205th MI Brigade had no organic interrogation elements; they had been eliminated by the downsizing in the 1990s. Soldiers from Army Reserve units filled the ranks, with the consequence that the Brigade Commander had to rely on disparate elements of units and individuals, including civilians, which had never trained together. The creation of the Joint Interrogation and Debriefing Center introduced another layer of complexity into an already stressed interrogations environment. The [center] was an ad hoc organization made up of six different units lacking the normal command and control structure, particularly at the senior noncommissioned officer level. Leadership was also lacking, from the Commander of the 800th MP Brigade in charge of Abu Ghraib, who failed to ensure that soldiers had appropriate standard operating procedures for dealing with detainees, to the Commander of the 205th MI Brigade, who failed to ensure that soldiers under his command were properly trained and followed the interrogation rules of engagement. Moreover, the Director of the Joint Interrogation and

Debriefing Center was a weak leader who did not have experience in interrogation operations and who ceded the core of his responsibilities to subordinates. He failed to provide appropriate training and supervision of personnel assigned to the Center. None of these leaders established the basic standards and accountability that might have served to prevent the abusive behaviors that occurred.

Interrogation Techniques

Interrogation techniques intended only for Guantanamo came to be used in Afghanistan and Iraq. Techniques employed at Guantanamo included the use of stress positions, isolation for up to 30 days and removal of clothing. In Afghanistan, techniques included removal of clothing, isolating people for long periods of time, use of stress positions, exploiting fear of dogs, and sleep and light deprivation. Interrogators in Iraq, already familiar with some of these ideas, implemented them even prior to any policy guidance from CJTF–7. Moreover, interrogators at Abu Ghraib were relying on a 1987 version of Field Manual 34–52, which authorized interrogators to control all aspects of the interrogation to include light, heating, food, clothing and shelter given to detainees.

A range of opinion among interrogators, staff judge advocates and commanders existed regarding what techniques were permissible. Some incidents of abuse were clearly cases of individual criminal misconduct. Other incidents resulted from misinterpretations of law or policy or confusion about what interrogation techniques were permitted by law or local standard operating procedures. The incidents stemming from misinterpretation or confusion occurred for several reasons: the proliferation of guidance and information from other theaters of operation; the interrogators' experiences in other theaters; and the failure to distinguish between permitted interrogation techniques in other theater environments and Iraq. Some soldiers or contractors who committed abuse may honestly have believed the techniques were condoned.

Use of Contractors as Interrogators

As a consequence of the shortage of interrogators and interpreters, contractors were used to augment the workforce. Contractors were a particular problem at Abu Ghraib. The Army Inspector General found that 35 percent of the contractors employed did not receive formal training in military interrogation techniques, policy, or doctrine. The Naval Inspector General, however, found some of the older contractors had backgrounds as former military interrogators and were generally considered more effective than some of the junior enlisted military personnel. Oversight of contractor personnel and activities was not sufficient to ensure intelligence operations fell within the law and the authorized chain of command. Continued use of contractors will be required, but contracts must clearly specify the technical requirements and personnel qualifications, experience, and training needed. They should also be developed and administered in such a way as to provide the necessary oversight and management.

Doctrinal Deficiencies

At the tactical level, detaining individuals primarily for intelligence collection or because they constitute a potential security threat, though necessary, presents units with situations not addressed by current doctrine. Many units adapted their operating procedures for conducting detainee operations to fit an environment not contemplated in the existing doctrinal manuals. The capturing units had no relevant procedures for information and evidence collection, which were critical for the proper disposition of detainees.

Additionally, there is inconsistent doctrine on interrogation facility operations for the fixed detention locations. Commanders had to improvise the organization and command relationships within these elements to meet the particular requirements of their operating environments in Afghanistan and Iraq. Doctrine is lacking to address the screening and interrogation of large numbers of detainees whose status (combatants, criminals, or innocents) is not easily ascertainable. Nor does policy specifically address administrative responsibilities related to the timely release of detainees captured and detained primarily for intelligence exploitation or for the security threat they may pose.

ROLE OF CIA

CIA personnel conducted interrogations in Department of Defense detention facilities. In some facilities these interrogations were conducted in conjunction with military personnel, but at Abu Ghraib the CIA was allowed to conduct its interrogations separately. No memorandum of understanding existed on interrogations operations between the CIA and CJTF–7, and the CIA was allowed to operate under different rules. According to the Fay investigation, the CIA's detention and interrogation practices contributed to a loss of accountability at Abu Ghraib. We are aware of the issue of unregistered detainees, but the Panel did not have sufficient access to CIA information to make any determinations in this regard.

THE ROLE OF MILITARY POLICE AND MILITARY INTELLIGENCE IN DETENTION OPERATIONS

Existing doctrine does not clearly address the relationship between the Military Police operating detention facilities and Military Intelligence personnel conducting intelligence exploitation at those facilities. The Army Inspector General report states neither MP nor MI doctrine specifically defines the distinct, but interdependent, roles and responsibilities of the two elements in detainee operations.

In the Global War on Terror, we are dealing with new conditions and new threats. Doctrine must be adjusted accordingly. MP doctrine currently states intelligence personnel may collaborate with MPs at detention sites to conduct interrogations, with coordination between the two groups to establish operating procedures. MP doctrine does not, however, address the subject of approved and prohibited MI procedures in an MP-operated facility. Conversely, MI doctrine does not clearly explain MP detention procedures or the role of MI personnel within a detention setting.

GUANTANAMO

The first detainees arrived at Guantanamo in January 2002. The Commander of the Southern Command established two Joint Task Forces at Guantanamo to execute the detention operations (Joint Task Force 160) and the interrogation operations (Joint Task Force 170). In August of that year, based on difficulties with the command relationships, the two Joint Task Forces were organized into a single command designated as Joint Task Force Guantanamo. This reorganization was conceived to enhance unity of command and direct all activities in support of interrogation and detention operations.

On November 4, 2002, Major General Miller was appointed Commander of Joint Task Force Guantanamo. As the joint commander, he called upon the MP and MI soldiers to work together cooperatively. Military police were to collect passive intelligence on detainees. They became key players, serving as the eyes and ears of the cellblocks for military intelligence personnel. This collaboration helped set conditions for successful interrogation by providing the interrogator more information about the detainee—his mood, his communications with other detainees, his receptivity to particular incentives, etc. Under the single command, the relationship between MPs and MIs became an effective operating model.

AFGHANISTAN

The MP and MI commands at the Bagram Detention Facility maintained separate chains of command and remained focused on their independent missions. The Combined Joint Task Force 76 Provost Marshal was responsible for detainee operations. He designated a principal assistant to run the Bagram facility. In parallel fashion, the CJTF–76 Intelligence Officer was responsible for MI operations in the facility, working through an Officer-in-Charge to oversee interrogation operations. The two deputies worked together to coordinate execution of their respective missions. A dedicated judge advocate was assigned full time to the facility, while the CJTF–76 Inspector General provided independent oversight. Based on information from the Naval Inspector General investigation, this arrangement in Afghanistan worked reasonably well.

ABU GHRAIB, IRAQ

The Central Confinement Facility is located near the population center of Baghdad. Abu Ghraib was selected by

Ambassador Bremer, who envisioned it as a temporary facility to be used for criminal detainees until the new Iraqi government could be established and an Iraqi prison established at another site. Following operations during the summer of 2003, Abu Ghraib also was designated by CJTF–7 as the detention center for security detainees. It was selected because it was difficult to transport prisoners, due to improvised explosive devices and other insurgent tactics, to the more remote and secure Camp Bucca, some 150 miles away.

Request for Assistance

Commander CJTF–7 recognized serious deficiencies at the prison and requested assistance. In response to this request, Major General Miller and a team from Guantanamo were sent to Iraq to provide advice on facilities and operations specific to screening, interrogations, human intelligence collection and interagency integration in the short- and long-term. The team arrived in Baghdad on August 31, 2003. Major General Miller brought a number of recommendations derived from his experience at Guantanamo, including his model for MP and MI personnel to work together. These collaborative procedures had worked well at Guantanamo, in part because of the high ratio of approximately one-to-one of military police to mostly compliant detainees. However, the guard-to-detainee ratio at Abu Ghraib was approximately 1 to 75, and the Military Intelligence and the Military Police had separate chains of command.

Major General Ryder, the Army Provost Marshal, also made an assistance visit in mid-October 2003. He conducted a review of detainee operations in Iraq. He found flawed operating procedures, a lack of training, an inadequate prisoner classification system, under-strength units and a ratio of guards to prisoners designed for "compliant" prisoners of war and not for criminals or high-risk security detainees. However, he failed to detect the warning signs of potential and actual abuse that was ongoing during his visit. The assessment team members did not identify any MP units purposely applying inappropriate confinement practices. The Ryder report continues that "Military Police, though adept at passive collection of intelligence within a facility, do not participate in Military Intelligence-supervised interrogation sessions. The 800th MP Brigade has not been asked to change its facility procedures to set the conditions for MI interviews, nor participate in those interviews."

Prevailing Conditions

Conditions at Abu Ghraib reflected an exception to those prevailing at other theater detainee facilities. U.S. forces were operating Tiers 1A and 1B, while Tiers 2 through 7 were under the complete control of Iraqi prison guards. Iraqis who had committed crimes against other Iraqis were intended to be housed in the tiers under Iraqi control. The facility was under frequent hostile fire from mortars and rocket-propelled grenades. Detainee escape attempts were numerous and there were several riots. Both MI and MP units were seriously under-resourced and lacked unit cohesion and mid-level leadership. The reserve MP units had lost senior non-commissioned officers and other personnel through rotations back to the U.S. as well as reassignments to other missions in the theater.

When Abu Ghraib opened, the first MP unit was the 72nd MP Company, based in Henderson, Nevada. Known as "the Nevada Company," it has been described by many involved in investigations concerning Abu Ghraib as a very strong unit that kept tight rein on operational procedures at the facility. This company called into question the interrogation practices of the MI brigade regarding nakedness of detainees. The 72nd MP Company voiced and then filed written objections to these practices.

The problems at Abu Ghraib intensified after October 15, 2003, when the 372nd Military Police Company took over the facility. The 372nd MP Company had been given the most sensitive mission: control of Tier 1A and Tier 1B, where civilian and military intelligence specialists held detainees identified for interrogations as well as "high-risk" detainees. An "MI Hold" was anyone of intelligence interest and included foreign and Iraqi terrorists, as well as individuals possessing information regarding foreign fighters, infiltration methods, or pending attacks on Coalition forces. The "high-risk" troublemakers were held in Tier lB. The prison cells of Tiers 1A and 1B were collectively known as "the hard site." The

372nd soldiers were not trained for prison guard duty and were thinly stretched in dealing with the large number of detainees. With little experience to fall back on, the company commander deferred to noncommissioned officers who had civilian correctional backgrounds to work the night shift. This deference was a significant error in judgment.

Leadership Shortfalls

At the leadership level, there was friction and a lack of communication between the 800th MP Brigade and the 205th MI Brigade through the summer and fall of 2003. There was no clear delineation of responsibility between commands and little coordination at the command level. Both the Director of the Joint Interrogation and Debriefing Center and the Commander of the 320th MP Battalion were weak and ineffective leaders. Both failed to ensure their subordinates were properly trained and supervised. They failed to establish and enforce basic soldier standards, proficiency, and accountability. Neither was able to organize tasks to accomplish their missions in an appropriate manner. By not communicating standards, policies, and plans to soldiers, these leaders conveyed a sense of tacit approval of abusive behaviors toward prisoners. This was particularly evident with respect to prisoner-handling procedures and techniques, including unfamiliarity with the Geneva Conventions. There was a lack of discipline and standards of behavior were not established nor enforced. A lax and dysfunctional command climate took hold.

In November 2003, the 205th MI Brigade Commander was assigned as the Forward Operation Base Commander, thus receiving responsibility for Abu Ghraib. This assignment was made as a result of CJTF–7 Commander's concern over force protection at the prison. The Fay investigation found this did not change the relationship of MP and MI units in day-to-day operations at the facility, although the Commander of the 800th MP Brigade says she was denied access to areas of Abu Ghraib for which she was doctrinally responsible. Key leaders did not seem to recognize or appreciate psychological stressors associated with the detention mission. Major General Taguba concluded these factors included "differences in culture, soldiers' quality of life, and the real presence of mortal danger over an extended time period. The failure of commanders to recognize these pressures contributed to the pervasive atmosphere existing at Abu Ghraib Detention Facility."

Military Working Dogs at Abu Ghraib

The Military Police directives give guidance for the use of military working dogs. They are used to provide an effective psychological and physical deterrent in the detention facility, offering an alternative to using firearms. Dogs are also used for perimeter security, inspections and patrols. Major General Miller had recommended dogs as beneficial for detainee custody and control during his visit in August/September 2003. However, he never recommended, nor were dogs used for interrogations at Guantanamo. The working dog teams were requested by the Commander 205th MI brigade who never understood the intent as described by Major General Miller. It is likely the confusion about using dogs partially stems from the initial request for dog teams by military intelligence and not military police.

The working dogs arrived at Abu Ghraib in mid-November 2003. The two Army teams were assigned primarily to security of the compound while the three Navy teams worked inside at the entry control point. The senior Army and Navy dog handlers indicated they had not previously worked in a prison environment and received only a one-day training session on scout and search for escaped Enemy Prisoners of War. The Navy handler stated that upon arrival at Abu Ghraib he had not received an orientation on what was expected from his canine unit nor what was authorized or not authorized. He further stated he had never received instruction on the use of force in the compound, but he acknowledged he knew a dog could not be used on a detainee if the detainee posed no threat.

Guidance provided by the CJTF–7 directive of September 14, 2003, allowed working dogs to be used as an interrogation technique with the CJTF–7 Commander's approval. This authorization was updated by the October 12, 2003, memorandum, which allowed the presence of dogs during interrogation as long as they were muzzled and under control of the handler at all times, but still required approval. The Taguba and Jones/Fay investigations identified a number of abuses related to using muzzled and unmuzzled dogs during interrogations. They also identified some abuses involving dog-use unrelated to interrogations, apparently for the sadistic pleasure of the MPs involved in these incidents.

MP/MI Relationship

It is clear, with these serious shortfalls and lack of supervision, the model Major General Miller presented for the effective working relationship between MI and MP was neither understood nor could it have been successfully implemented. Based on the Taguba and Jones/Fay investigations, "setting favorable conditions" had some basis in fact at Abu Ghraib, but it was also used as an excuse for abusive behavior toward detainees.

The events that took place at Abu Ghraib are an aberration when compared to the situations at other detention operations. Poor leadership and a lack of oversight set the stage for abuses to occur.

LAWS OF WAR/GENEVA CONVENTIONS

American military culture, training, and operations are steeped in a long-held commitment to the tenets of military and international law as traditionally codified by the world community. Department of Defense Directive 5100.77, Department of Defense Law of War Program, describes the law of war as:

> That part of international law that regulates the conduct of armed hostilities. It is often called the law of armed conflict. The law of war encompasses all international law for the conduct of hostilities binding on the United States or its individual citizens, including treaties and international agreements to which the United States is a party, and applicable customary international law.

The law of war includes, among other agreements, the Geneva Conventions of 1949. The Geneva Conventions set forth the rights and obligations which govern the treatment of civilians and combatants during periods of armed conflict. Specifically, Geneva Convention III addresses the treatment of prisoners of war; and Geneva Convention IV addresses the treatment of civilians.

Chairman of the Joint Chiefs of Staff Instruction 5810.01 B, Implementation of the Department of Defense Law of War Program, reiterates U.S. policy concerning the law of war: "The Armed Forces of the United States will comply with the law of war during all armed conflicts, however such conflicts are characterized. . . . "

The United States became engaged in two distinct conflicts, Operation Enduring Freedom in Afghanistan and Operation Iraqi Freedom in Iraq. As a result of a Presidential determination, the Geneva Conventions did not apply to Al-Qaeda and Taliban combatants. Nevertheless, these traditional standards were put into effect for Operation Iraqi Freedom and remain in effect at this writing. Some would argue this is a departure from the traditional view of the law of war as espoused by the International Committee of the Red Cross and others in the international community.

Operation Enduring Freedom

On October 17, 2001, pursuant to the commencement of combat operations in Operation Enduring Freedom, the Commander, Central Command, issued an order instructing the Geneva Conventions were to be applied to all captured individuals in accordance with their traditional interpretation. Belligerents would be screened to determine whether or not they were entitled to prisoner of war status. If an individual was entitled to prisoner of war status, the protections of Geneva Convention III would apply. If armed forces personnel were in doubt as to a detained individual's status, Geneva Convention III rights would be accorded to the detainee until a Geneva Convention III Article 5 tribunal made a definitive status determination. If the individual was found not to be entitled to Geneva Convention III protections, he or she might be detained and processed under U.S. criminal code, a procedure consistent with Geneva Convention IV.

A policy debate concerning the application of treaties

and laws to Al-Qaeda and Taliban detainees then began taking shape. The Department of Justice Office of Legal Counsel provided opinions to Counsel to the President and Department of Defense General Counsel concluding the Geneva Conventions did not protect members of the Al-Qaeda organization, and the President could decide that the Geneva Conventions did not protect Taliban militia. Counsel to the President and the Attorney General so advised the President.

On February 7, 2002, the President issued a memorandum stating, in part,

> ...the war against terrorism ushers in a new paradigm.... Our nation recognizes that this new paradigm—ushered in not by us, but by terrorists—requires new thinking in the law of war, but thinking that should nevertheless be consistent with the principles of Geneva.

Upon this premise, the President determined the Geneva Conventions did not apply to the U.S. conflict with Al-Qaeda, and that Taliban detainees did not qualify for prisoner of war status. Removed from the protections of the Geneva Conventions, Al-Qaeda and Taliban detainees have been classified variously as "unlawful combatants," "enemy combatants," and "unprivileged belligerents."

The enemy in the Global War on Terror is one neither the United States nor the community of nations has ever before engaged on such an extensive scale. These far-reaching, well-resourced, organized, and trained terrorists are attempting to achieve their own ends. Such terrorists are not of a nation state such as those who are party to the agreements which comprise the law of war. Neither do they conform their actions to the letter or spirit of the law of war.

The Panel accepts the proposition that these terrorists are not combatants entitled to the protections of Geneva Convention III. Furthermore, the Panel accepts the conclusion that the Geneva Convention IV and the provisions of domestic criminal law are not sufficiently robust and adequate to provide for the appropriate detention of captured terrorists.

The Panel notes the President qualified his determination, directing that United States policy would be "consistent with the principles of Geneva." Among other things, the Geneva Conventions adhere to a standard calling for a delineation of rights for all persons, and humane treatment for all persons. They suggest that no person is "outlaw," that is, outside the laws of some legal entity.

The Panel finds the details of the current policy vague and lacking. Justice Sandra Day O'Connor, writing for the majority in *Hamdi v Rumsfeld*, June 28, 2004, points out "the Government has never provided any court with the full criteria that it uses in classifying individuals as [enemy combatants]." Justice O'Connor cites several authorities to support the proposition that detention "is a clearly established principle of the law of war," but also states there is no precept of law, domestic or international, which would permit the indefinite detention of any combatant.

As a matter of logic, there should be a category of persons who do not comply with the specified conditions and thus fall outside the category of persons entitled to Enemy Prisoner of War status. Although there is not a particular label for this category in law of war conventions, the concept of "unlawful combatant" or "unprivileged belligerent" is a part of the law of war.

Operation Iraqi Freedom

Operation Iraqi Freedom is wholly different from Operation Enduring Freedom. It is an operation that clearly falls within the boundaries of the Geneva Conventions and the traditional law of war. From the very beginning of the campaign, none of the senior leadership or command considered any possibility other than that the Geneva Conventions applied.

The message in the field, or the assumptions made in the field, at times lost sight of this underpinning. Personnel familiar with the law of war determinations for Operation Enduring Freedom in Afghanistan tended to factor those determinations into their decision-making for military actions in Iraq. Law of war policy and decisions germane to Operation Enduring Freedom migrated, often quite innocently, into decision matrices for Operation

Iraqi Freedom. We noted earlier the migration of interrogation techniques from Afghanistan to Iraq. Those interrogation techniques were authorized only for Operation Enduring Freedom. More important, their authorization in Afghanistan and Guantanamo was possible only because the President had determined that individuals subjected to these interrogation techniques fell outside the strict protections of the Geneva Conventions.

One of the more telling examples of this migration centers around CJTF–7's determination that some of the detainees held in Iraq were to be categorized as unlawful combatants. "Unlawful combatants" was a category set out in the President's February 7, 2002, memorandum. Despite lacking specific authorization to operate beyond the confines of the Geneva Conventions, CJTF–7 nonetheless determined it was within their command discretion to classify, as unlawful combatants, individuals captured during Operation Iraqi Freedom. CJTF–7 concluded it had individuals in custody who met the criteria for unlawful combatants set out by the President and extended it in Iraq to those who were not protected as combatants under the Geneva Conventions, based on the Office of Legal Counsel opinions. While CJTF–7's reasoning is understandable in respect to unlawful combatants, nonetheless, they understood there was no authorization to suspend application of the Geneva Conventions, in letter and spirit, to all military actions of Operation Iraqi Freedom. In addition, CJTF–7 had no means of discriminating detainees among the various categories of those protected under the Geneva Conventions and those unlawful combatants who were not.

THE ROLE OF THE INTERNATIONAL COMMITTEE OF THE RED CROSS

Since December 2001, the International Committee of the Red Cross (ICRC) has visited U.S. detention operations in Guantanamo, Iraq, and Afghanistan numerous times. Various ICRC inspection teams have delivered working papers and reports of findings to U.S. military leaders at different levels. While the ICRC has acknowledged U.S. attempts to improve the conditions of detainees, major differences over detainee status as well as application of specific provisions of Geneva Conventions III and IV remain. If we were to follow the ICRC's interpretations, interrogation operations would not be allowed. This would deprive the U.S. of an indispensable source of intelligence in the war on terrorism.

The ICRC is an independent agency whose activities include observing and reporting on conditions in wartime detention camps and facilities. During visits, it attempts to register all prisoners, inspect facilities, and conduct private interviews with detainees to discuss any problems concerning detainee treatment or conditions; it also provides a means for detainees to contact their families. While the ICRC has no enforcing authority and its reports are supposedly confidential, any public revelation regarding standards of detainee treatment can have a substantial effect on international opinion.

The ICRC seeks to handle problems at the lowest level possible. When a team conducts an inspection, it provides a briefing, and sometimes a report, to the local commander. Discrepancies and issues are presented to the detaining authorities, and follow-up visits are made to monitor compliance with recommendations. The commander may or may not implement the recommendations based on either resource constraint or his interpretation of applicable law. These constraints can make complete implementation of ICRC recommendations either difficult or inappropriate. If recommendations are not implemented, the ICRC may address the issue with higher authorities. The ICRC does not expect to receive, nor does the Department of Defense have a policy of providing, a written response to ICRC reports. However, Department of Defense elements do attempt to implement as many of the recommendations as practicable, given security and resource constraints.

One important difference in approach between the U.S. and the ICRC is the interpretation of the legal status of terrorists. According to a Panel interview with CJTF–7 legal counsel, the ICRC sent a report to the State Department and the Coalition Provisional Authority in February 2003 citing lack of compliance with Protocol 1. But the U.S. has specifically rejected Protocol 1, stating that certain elements in the protocol, that provide legal protection for terrorists, make it plainly unacceptable. Still the

U.S. has worked to preserve the positive elements of Protocol 1. In 1985, the Secretary of Defense noted that "certain provisions of Protocol 1 reflect customary international law, and others appear to be positive new developments. We therefore intend to work with our allies and others to develop a common understanding or declaration of principles incorporating these positive aspects, with the intention they shall, in time, win recognition as customary international law." In 1986 the ICRC acknowledged that it and the U.S. government had "agreed to disagree" on the applicability of Protocol 1. Nevertheless, the ICRC continues to presume the United States should adhere to this standard under the guise of customary international law.

This would grant legal protections to terrorists equivalent to the protections accorded to prisoners of war as required by the Geneva Conventions of 1949 despite the fact terrorists do not wear uniforms and are otherwise indistinguishable from noncombatants. To do so would undermine the prohibition on terrorists blending in with the civilian population, a situation which makes it impossible to attack terrorists without placing noncombatants at risk. For this and other reasons, the U.S. has specifically rejected this additional protocol.

The ICRC also considers the U.S. policy of categorizing some detainees as "unlawful combatants" to be a violation of their interpretation of international humanitarian law. It contends that Geneva Conventions III and IV, which the U.S. has ratified, allow for only two categories of detainees: (1) civilian detainees who must be charged with a crime and tried, and (2) enemy combatants who must be released at the cessation of hostilities. In the ICRC's view, the category of "unlawful combatant" deprives the detainees of certain human rights. It argues that lack of information regarding the reasons for detention and the conditions for release are major sources of stress for detainees.

However, the 1949 Geneva Conventions specify conditions to qualify for protected status. By logic, then, if detainees do not meet the specific requirements of privileged status, there clearly must be a category for those lacking in such privileges. The ICRC does not acknowledge such a category of "unprivileged belligerents," and argues that it is not consistent with its interpretation of the Geneva Conventions.

Regarding the application of current international humanitarian law, including Geneva Conventions III and IV, the ICRC has three concerns: (1) gaining access to and ascertaining the status of all detainees in U.S. custody; (2) its belief that linking detention with interrogations should not be allowed, which follows from its refusal to recognize the category of unprivileged combatants; and (3) they also worry about losing their effectiveness.

Although the ICRC found U.S. forces generally cooperative, it has cited occasions when the forces did not grant adequate access to detainees, both in Iraq and Afghanistan. Of particular concern to the ICRC, however, has been the existence of "ghost detainees," detainees who were kept from ICRC inspectors. While the Panel has not been able to ascertain the number of ghost detainees in the overall detainee population, several investigations cite their existence. Both the Taguba and Jones/Fay reports cite instances of ghost detainees at Abu Ghraib. Secretary Rumsfeld publicly declared he directed one detainee be held secretly at the request of the Director of Central Intelligence.

On balance, the Panel concludes there is value in the relationship the Department of Defense historically has had with the ICRC. The ICRC should serve as an early warning indicator of possible abuse. Commanders should be alert to ICRC observations in their reports and take corrective actions as appropriate. The Panel also believes the ICRC, no less than the Defense Department, needs to adapt itself to the new realities of conflict, which are far different from the Western European environment from which the ICRC's interpretation of Geneva Conventions was drawn. The Department of Defense has established an office of detainee affairs and should continue to reshape its operational relationship with the ICRC.

RECOMMENDATIONS

Department of Defense reform efforts are underway and the Panel commends these efforts. The Office of the Secretary of Defense, the Joint Chiefs of Staff and the Military Services are conducting comprehensive reviews on how military operations have changed since the end of the Cold War. The military services now recognize the problems and are studying how to adjust force compositions, training, doctrine and responsibilities for active/reserve/guard and contractor mixes to ensure we are better prepared to succeed in the war on terrorism.

The Panel reviewed various inspections, investigations and assessments that produced over 300 recommendations for corrective actions to address the problems identified with Department of Defense detention operations. For the most part the Panel endorses their recommendations. In some areas the recommendations do not go far enough and we augment them. We provide additional recommendations to address relevant areas not covered by previous analyses.

The Independent Panel provides the following additional recommendations:

1.   The United States should further define its policy, applicable to both the Department of Defense and other government agencies, on the categorization and status of all detainees as it applies to various operations and theaters. It should define their status and treatment in a way consistent with U.S. jurisprudence and military doctrine and with U.S. interpretation of the Geneva Conventions. We recommend that additional operational, support and staff judge advocate personnel be assigned to appropriate commands for the purpose of expediting the detainee release review process.

2.   The Department of Defense needs to address and develop joint doctrine to define the appropriate collaboration between military intelligence and military police in a detention facility. The meaning of guidance, such as MPs "setting the conditions" for interrogation, needs to be defined with precision. Major General Taguba argued that all detainee operations be consolidated under the responsibility of a single commander reporting directly to Commander CJTF–7. This change has now been accomplished and seems to be working effectively. Other than lack of leadership, training deficiencies in both MP and MI units have been cited most often as the needed measures to prevent detainee abuse. We support the recommendations on training articulated by the reports published by the various other reviews.

3.   The nation needs more specialists for detention/ interrogation operations, including linguists, interrogators, human intelligence, counter-intelligence, corrections police and behavioral scientists. Accompanying professional development and career field management systems must be put in place concurrently. The Panel agrees that some use of contractors in detention operations must continue into the foreseeable future. This is especially the case with the need for qualified interpreters and interrogators and will require rigorous oversight.

4.   Joint Forces Command should chair a Joint Service Integrated Process Team to develop a new

Operational Concept for Detention Operations in the new era of warfare, covering the Global War on Terror. The team should place special and early emphasis on detention operations during Counter-Insurgency campaigns and Stability Operations in which familiar concepts of front and rear areas may not apply. Attention should also be given to preparing for conditions in which normal law enforcement has broken down in an occupied or failed state. The Panel recommends that the idea of a deployable detention facility should be studied and implemented as appropriate.

5.   Clearly, force structure in both MP and MI is inadequate to support the armed forces in this new form of warfare. Every investigation we reviewed refers to force structure deficiencies in some measure. There should be an active and reserve component mix of units for both military intelligence and military police. Other forces besides the Army are also in need of force structure improvements. Those forces have not been addressed adequately in the reports reviewed by the Panel, and we recommend that the Secretaries of the Navy and Air Force undertake force structure reviews of their own to improve the performance of their Services in detention operations.

6.   Well-documented policy and procedures on approved interrogation techniques are imperative to counteract the current chilling effect the reac-

tion to the abuses have had on the collection of valuable intelligence through interrogations. Given the critical role of intelligence in the Global War on Terror, the aggressiveness of interrogation techniques employed must be measured against the value of intelligence sought, to include its importance, urgency and relevance. A policy for interrogation operations should be promulgated early on, and acceptable interrogation techniques for each operation must be clearly understood by all interrogation personnel.

7. All personnel who may be engaged in detention operations, from point of capture to final disposition, should participate in a professional ethics program that would equip them with a sharp moral compass for guidance in situations often riven with conflicting moral obligations. The development of such a values-oriented ethics program should be the responsibility of the individual services with assistance provided by the Joint Chiefs of Staff.

8. Clearer guidelines for the interaction of CIA with the Department of Defense in detention and interrogation operations must be defined.

9. The United States needs to redefine its approach to customary and treaty international humanitarian law, which must be adapted to the realities of the nature of conflict in the 21st century. In doing so, the United States should emphasize the stan-

dard of reciprocity, in spite of the low probability that such will be extended to United States forces by some adversaries, and the preservation of United States societal values and international image that flows from an adherence to recognized humanitarian standards.

10. The Department of Defense should continue to foster its operational relationship with the International Committee of the Red Cross. The Panel believes the International Committee of the Red Cross, no less than the Defense Department, needs to adapt itself to the new realities of conflict, which are far different from the Western European environment from which the ICRC's interpretation of Geneva Conventions was drawn.

11. The assignment of a focal point within the office of the Under Secretary for Policy would be a useful organizational step. The new focal point for Detainee Affairs should be charged with all aspects of detention policy and also be responsible for oversight of Department of Defense relations with the International Committee of the Red Cross.

12. The Secretary of Defense should ensure the effective functioning of rapid reporting channels for communicating bad news to senior Department of Defense leadership without prejudice to any criminal or disciplinary actions already underway. The Panel recommends consideration of a joint adap-

tation of procedures such as the Air Force special notification process.

13.   The Panel notes that the Fay investigation cited some medical personnel for failure to report detainee abuse. As noted in that investigation, training should include the obligation to report any detainee abuse. The Panel also notes that the Army Inspector General found significant shortfalls in training and force structure for field sanitation, preventive medicine and medical treatment requirements for detainees. As the Department of Defense improves detention operations force structure and training, it should pay attention to the need for medical personnel to screen and monitor the health of detention personnel and detainees.

14.   The integration of the recommendations in this report and all the other efforts underway on detention operations will require further study. Analysis of the dynamics of program and resource implications, with a view to assessing the trade-offs and opportunity costs involved, must be addressed.

Charles A. Graner and Sabrina Harman pose behind a pyramid of naked
Iraqi prisoners.

Lynndie England points at the genitals of hooded prisoners forced to stand
in line.

Lynndie England holds what appears to be a dog's leash around naked detainee's neck.

American military dog handlers and an Iraqi prisoner.

An unidentified U.S. soldier appears prepared to punch a detainee as other detainees lie bound at the hands.

A U.S. soldier, baton in hand, stands guard over a naked Iraqi detainee cuffed at the ankles and covered in a brown substance.

A hooded Iraqi detainee forced to stand balanced on two boxes.

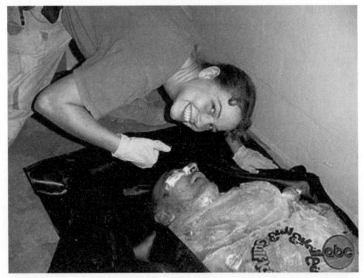

Sabrina Harman smiles and gives a thumbs-up sign by the body of Iraqi detainee Manadel al-Jamadi.

Investigation of the Abu Ghraib Detention Facility and 205th Military Intelligence Brigade

———

Investigation of the Abu Ghraib Detention Facility and 205th Military Intelligence Brigade

Maj. Gen. George R. Fay, Investigating Officer

This investigation identified 44 alleged instances or events of detainee abuse committed by Military Police (MP) and Military Intelligence (MI) soldiers, as well as civilian contractors. On 16 of these occasions, abuse by the MP soldiers was, or was alleged to have been, requested, encouraged, condoned, or solicited by MI personnel. The abuse, however, was directed on an individual basis and never officially sanctioned or approved. ...In 11 instances, MI personnel were found to be directly involved in the abuse. MI personnel were also found not to have fully comported with established interrogation procedures and applicable laws and regulations. Theater Interrogation and Counter-Resistance Policies were found to be poorly defined, and changed several times. As a result, interrogation activities sometimes crossed into abusive activity. . . .

Leaders in key positions failed properly to supervise the interrogation operations at Abu Ghraib and failed to understand the dynamics created at Abu Ghraib. Leaders also failed to react appropriately to those instances where detainee abuse was reported, whether by other service members, contractors, or by the International Committee of the Red Cross. Fifty-four MI, MP, and Medical soldiers, and civilian contractors were found to have some degree of responsibility or complicity in the abuses that occurred at Abu Ghraib. Twenty-seven were cited in this report for some degree of culpability and 17 were cited for misunderstanding of policy, regulation or law. Three MI soldiers, who had previously received punishment under the Uniform Code of Military Justice (UCMJ), were recommended for additional investigation. Seven MP soldiers identified in the Maj. Gen. [Antonio] Taguba Report and currently under criminal investigation and/or charges are also central figures in this investigation and are included in the above numbers. One person cited in the Taguba Report was exonerated.

Looking beyond personal responsibility, leader responsibility and command responsibility, systemic problems and issues also contributed to the volatile environment in which the abuse occurred. These systemic problems included: inadequate interrogation doctrine and training, an acute shortage of MP and MI soldiers, the lack of clear lines of responsibility between the MP and MI chains of command, the lack of a clear interrogation policy for the Iraq Campaign, and intense pressure felt by the personnel on the ground to produce actionable intelligence from detainees....

The CIA [commonly referred to as "other government agencies"] conducted unilateral and joint interrogation operations at Abu Ghraib. The CIA's detention and interrogation practices contributed to a loss of accountability and abuse at Abu Ghraib. No memorandum of understanding existed on the subject interrogation operations between the CIA and CJTF–7 [Combined Joint Task Force 7, the forward-deployed military headquarters for Iraq]. Local CIA officers convinced military leaders that they should be allowed to operate outside the established local rules and procedures. CIA detainees in Abu Ghraib, known locally as "Ghost Detainees," were not accounted for in the detention system. With these detainees unidentified or unaccounted for, . . . personnel at the operations level were uncertain how to report or classify detainees.

SUMMARY OF ABUSES AT ABU GHRAIB

Several types of detainee abuse were identified in this investigation: physical and sexual abuse; improper use of military working dogs; humiliating and degrading treatments; and improper use of isolation.

1. PHYSICAL ABUSE. Several soldiers reported that they witnessed physical abuse of detainees. Some examples include slapping, kicking, twisting the

hands of a detainee who was handcuffed to cause pain, throwing balls at restrained internees, placing a gloved hand over the nose and mouth of an internee to restrict breathing, "poking" at an internee's injured leg, and forcing an internee to stand while handcuffed in such a way as to dislocate his shoulder. These actions are clearly in violation of applicable laws and regulations.

2. USE OF DOGS. The use of military working dogs in a confinement facility can be effective and permissible ... as a means of controlling the internee population. When dogs are used to threaten and terrify detainees, there is a clear violation of applicable laws and regulations. One such impermissible practice was an alleged contest between the two Army dog handlers to see who could make the internees urinate or defecate in the presence of the dogs. An incident of clearly abusive use of the dogs occurred when a dog was allowed in the cell of two male juveniles and allowed to go "nuts." Both juveniles were screaming and crying, with the youngest and smallest trying to hide behind the other juvenile.

3. HUMILIATING AND DEGRADING TREATMENTS. Actions that are intended to degrade or humiliate a detainee are prohibited by Geneva Convention IV, Army policy and UCMJ. The following are examples of such behavior that occurred at Abu Ghraib, which violate applicable laws and regulations.

4. NAKEDNESS. Numerous statements, as well as the report by the International Committee of the Red Cross, discuss the seemingly common practice of keeping detainees in a state of undress. A number of statements indicate that clothing was taken away as a punishment for either not cooperating with interrogators or with MPs. In addition, male internees were naked in the presence of female soldiers. Many of the soldiers who witnessed the nakedness were told that this was an accepted practice. Under the circumstances, however, the nakedness was clearly degrading and humiliating.

5. PHOTOGRAPHS. A multitude of photographs show detainees in various states of undress, often in degrading positions.

6. SIMULATED SEXUAL POSITIONS. A number of soldiers describe incidents where detainees were placed in simulated sexual positions with other internees. Many of these incidents were also photographed.

7. IMPROPER USE OF ISOLATION. There are some legitimate purposes for the segregation (or isolation) of detainees, specifically to prevent them from sharing interrogation tactics with other detainees or other sensitive information. Article 5 of Geneva Convention IV supports this position by stating that certain individuals can lose their rights of communication, but only when absolute military security requires. The use of isolation at

Abu Ghraib was often done as punishment, either
for a disciplinary infraction or for failure to cooperate with an interrogation. These are improper
uses of isolation and depending on the circumstances amounted to violation of applicable laws
and regulations. Isolation could properly be a
sanction for a disciplinary infraction if applied
through the proper process ... and the Geneva
Conventions.

8. FAILURE TO SAFEGUARD DETAINEES. The Geneva
Conventions and Army Regulations require that
detainees be "protected against all acts of violence
and threats thereof and against insults and public
curiosity." ... The duty to protect imposes an obligation on an individual who witnesses an abusive
act to intervene and stop the abuse. Failure to do
so may be a violation of applicable laws and regulations.

9. FAILURE TO REPORT DETAINEE ABUSE. The duty to
report detainee abuse is closely tied to the duty to
protect. The failure to report an abusive incident
could result in additional abuse. Soldiers who wit-
ness these offenses have an obligation to report
the violations under the provision of Article 92,
UCMJ. Soldiers who are informed of such abuses
also have a duty to report violations. Depending
on their position and their assigned duties, the
failure to report detainee abuse could support a
charge of dereliction of duty, a violation of the

UCMJ. Civilian contractors employed as interrogators and translators would also have a duty to
report such offenses as they are also bound by the
Geneva Conventions and are charged with pro-
tecting the internees.

Other traditional prison guard issues were far less
clear. MPs are responsible for the clothing of detainees;
however, MI interrogators started directing nakedness at
Abu Ghraib as early as 16 September 2003 to humiliate
and break down detainees. MPs would also sometimes
discipline detainees by taking away clothing and putting
detainees in cells naked. A severe shortage of clothing
during the September, October, November, 2003 time
frame was frequently mentioned as the reason why people were naked. Removal of clothing and nakedness were
being used to humiliate detainees at the same time there
was a general level of confusion as to what was allowable
in terms of MP disciplinary measures and MI interrogation rules, and what clothing was available. This contributed to an environment that would appear to
condone depravity and degradation rather than the
humane treatment of detainees.

The original intent by MI leadership (205 MI Brigade)
was for Tier 1A to be reserved for MI Holds only. In fact,
Captain Wood states in an email dated 7 September
2003, during a visit from Maj. Gen. [Geoffrey] Miller
and Brig. Gen. [Janis] Karpinski, that Brigadier General
Karpinski confirmed "we [MI] have all the iso [isolation]

cells in the wing we have been working. We only had 10 cells to begin with but that has grown to the entire wing." Lt. Col. [Jerry] Phillabaum also thought that MI had exclusive authority to house MI Holds in Tier 1A. The fact is, however, that a number of those cells were often used by the MPs to house disciplinary problems. That fact is supported by the testimony of a large number of people who were there and further supported by the pictures and the detainee records. In fact, 11 of a total of 25 detainees identified by the Criminal Investigation Command (CID) as victims of abuse were not MI Holds and were not being interrogated by MI. The MPs put the problem detainees (detainees who required separation from the general population for disciplinary reasons) in Tier 1A because there was no other place available to isolate them. Neither Captain Wood nor Major Williams appreciated the mixing because it did not allow for a pure MI environment, but the issue never made its way up to either Lieutenant Colonel Phillabaum or to Brigadier General Karpinski.

The "sleep adjustment" technique was used by MI as soon as the Tier 1A block opened. This was another source of confusion and misunderstanding between MPs and MI which contributed to an environment that allowed detainee abuse, as well as its perpetuation for as long as it continued. Sleep adjustment was brought with the 519 MI Battalion from Afghanistan. It is also a method used at Guantanamo. At Abu Ghraib, however, the MPs were not trained, nor informed as to how they actually should do the sleep adjustment. The MPs were just told to keep a detainee awake for a time specified by the interrogator. The MPs used their own judgment as to how to keep them awake. Those techniques included taking the detainees out of their cells, stripping them and giving them cold showers. Captain Wood stated she did not know this was going on and thought the detainees were being kept awake by the MPs banging on the cell doors, yelling, and playing loud music. When one MI soldier inquired about water being thrown on a naked detainee he was told that it was an MP discipline technique. Again, who was allowed to do what and how exactly they were to do it was totally unclear. Neither of the communities (MI and MP) knew what the other could and could not do.

This investigation found no evidence of confusion regarding actual physical abuse, such as hitting, kicking, slapping, punching, and foot stomping. Everyone we spoke to knew it was prohibited conduct except for one soldier. Physical discomfort from exposure to cold and heat or denial of food and water is not as clear-cut and can become physical or moral coercion at the extreme. Such abuse did occur at Abu Ghraib, such as detainees being left naked in their cells during severe cold weather without blankets. In Tier 1A some of the excesses regarding physical discomfort were being done as directed by MI and some were being done by MPs for reasons not related to interrogation.

The physical and sexual abuses of detainees at Abu

Ghraib are by far the most serious. The abuses spanned from direct physical assault, such as delivering head blows rendering detainees unconscious, to sexual posing and forced participation in group masturbation. At the extremes were the death of a detainee in OGA [Other Government Agency] custody, an alleged rape committed by a U.S. translator and observed by a female soldier, and the alleged sexual assault of an unknown female. They were perpetrated or witnessed by individuals or small groups. Such abuse can not be directly tied to a systemic U.S. approach to torture or approved treatment of detainees. The MPs being investigated claim their actions came at the direction of MI. Although self-serving, these claims do have some basis in fact. The climate created at Abu Ghraib provided the opportunity for such abuse to occur and to continue undiscovered by higher authority for a long period of time. What started as undressing and humiliation, stress and physical training, carried over into sexual and physical assaults by a small group of morally corrupt and unsupervised soldiers and civilians. Twenty-four serious incidents of physical and sexual abuse occurred from 20 September through 13 December 2003.

INCIDENT No. 1. On 20 September 2003, two MI soldiers beat and kicked a passive, cuffed detainee, suspected of involvement in the 20 September 2003 mortar attack on Abu Ghraib that killed two soldiers. Two Iraqis (male and female) were detained and brought to Abu Ghraib immediately following the attack. MI and the MP Internal Reaction Force (IRF) were notified of the apprehension and dispatched teams to the entry control point to receive the detainees. Upon arrival, the IRF observed two MI soldiers striking and yelling at the male detainee, whom they subsequently "threw" into the back of a High-Mobility Multipurpose Wheeled Vehicle. First Lieutenant Sutton, 320th MP Battalion IRF, intervened to stop the abuse and was told by the MI soldiers "we are the professionals; we know what we are doing." They refused First Lieutenant Sutton's lawful order to identify themselves. First Lieutenant Sutton and his IRF team (Sergeant Spiker, Sergeant First Class Plude) immediately reported this incident, providing sworn statements to Major Dinenna, 320 MP Battalion S3, and Lieutenant Colonel Phillabaum, 320 MP Battalion Commander. First Sergeant McBride, A/205 MI Battalion, interviewed and took statements from Sergeant Lawson, identified as striking the detainee, and each MI person present: Staff Sergeant Hannifan, Staff Sergeant Cole, Sergeant Claus, Sergeant Presnell. While the MP statements all describe abuse at the hands of an unidentified MI person (Sergeant Lawson), the MI statements all deny any abuse occurred. Lieutenant Colonel Phillabaum subsequently reported the incident to the CID, who determined the allegation lacked sufficient basis for prosecution. The detainee was interrogated and released that day (involvement in the mortar attack was unlikely); therefore, no detainee is available to confirm either the MP or MI recollection of events. This incident was not further pursued based on limited data and the absence of additional investigative leads.

INCIDENT NO. 2. On 7 October 2003, three MI personnel allegedly sexually assaulted female Detainee–29. Civilian–06 [employed by contractor Titan Corporation] was the assigned interpreter, but there is no indication he was present or involved. Detainee–29 alleges as follows: First, the group took her out of her cell and escorted her down the cellblock to an empty cell. One unidentified soldier stayed outside the cell (Soldier–33, A/519 MI Battalion), while another held her hands behind her back, and the other forcibly kissed her (Soldier–32, A/519 MI Battalion). She was escorted downstairs to another cell where she was shown a naked male detainee and told the same would happen to her if she did not cooperate. She was then taken back to her cell and forced to kneel and raise her arms while one of the soldiers (Soldier–31, A/519 MI Battalion) removed her shirt. She began to cry, and her shirt was given back as the soldier cursed at her and said they would be back each night. CID conducted an investigation and Soldier–33, Soldier–32, and Soldier–31 invoked their rights and refused to provide any statements. Detainee–29 identified Soldier–33, Soldier–32, and Soldier–31 as the soldiers who kissed her and removed her shirt. Checks with the 519 MI Battalion confirmed no interrogations were scheduled for that evening. No record exists of MI ever conducting an authorized interrogation of her. The CID investigation was closed. Soldier–33, Soldier–32, and Soldier–31 each received non-judicial punishment ... from the Commander, 205 MI Brigade, for failing to get authorization to interrogate Detainee–29. Additionally, Col. [Thomas] Pappas removed them from interrogation operations.

INCIDENT NO. 3. On 25 October 2003 detainees Detainee–31, Detainee–30, and Detainee–27 were stripped of their clothing, handcuffed together nude, placed on the ground, and forced to lie on each other and simulate sex while photographs were taken. Six photographs depict this abuse. Results of the CID investigation indicate that on several occasions over several days detainees were assaulted, abused and forced to strip off their clothing and perform indecent acts on each other. Detainee–27 provided a sworn statement outlining these abuses. Those present and/or participating in the abuse were Corporal Graner, 372 MP Company, Staff Sergeant Frederick, 372 MP Company, Specialist England, 372 MP Company, Specialist Harman, 372 MP Company, Soldier–34, 372 MP Company, Civilian–17, Titan Corp., Soldier–24, B/325 MI Battalion, Soldier–19, 325 MI Battalion, and Soldier–10, 325 MI Battalion. Soldier–24 claimed he accompanied Soldier–10 to the Hard Site the evening of 25 October 2003 to see what was being done to the three detainees suspected of raping a young male detainee. Soldier–10 appeared to have foreknowledge of the abuse, possibly from his friendship with Specialist Harman, a 372 MP Company MP. Soldier–24 did not believe the abuse was directed by MI and these individuals were not interrogation subjects. Private First Class England, however, claimed "MI soldiers instructed them (MPs) to rough them up." When Soldier–24 arrived the detainees were naked, being yelled at by an MP through a megaphone. The detainees were forced to crawl on their stomachs and were handcuffed together. Soldier–24 observed Soldier–10 join in the abuse with Corporal Graner and Staff Sergeant Frederick. All three made the detainees act as though they were having sex. He observed Soldier–19 dump water on the detainees from a cup and throw a foam football at them. Soldier–24 described what he saw to Soldier–25, B/321 MI Battalion, who reported the incident to Sergeant Joyner, 372 MP Company. Sergeant Joyner advised Soldier–25 he would notify his Non-Commissioned Officer in Charge and later told Soldier–25 "he had taken care of it." Soldier–25 stated that a few days later both she and Soldier–24 told Soldier–22 of the incident. Soldier–22 subsequently failed to report what he was told. Soldier–25 did not report the abuse through MI channels because she felt it was an MP matter and would be handled by them.

This is a clear incident of direct MI personnel involvement in detainee abuse; however, it does not appear to be based on MI orders. The three detainees were incarcerated for criminal acts and were not of intelligence interest. This incident was most likely orchestrated by MP personnel (Corporal Graner, Staff Sergeant Frederick, Soldier–34, Specialist Harman, Private First Class England), with the MI personnel (Soldier–19, Soldier–10, and Soldier–24), Civilian–17, and another unidentified interpreter joining in and/or observing the abuse.

INCIDENT NO. 4. Detainee–08, arrived at Abu Ghraib on 27 October 2003 and was subsequently sent to the Hard Site. Detainee–08 claims when he was sent to the Hard Site, he was stripped of his clothing for six days. He was then given a blanket and remained with only the blanket for three more days. Detainee–08 stated the next evening he was transported by Corporal Graner, 372 MP Company, to the shower room, which was commonly used for interrogations. When the interrogation ended, his female interrogator left, and Detainee–08 claims Corporal Graner and another MP, who meets the description of Staff Sergeant Frederick, then threw pepper in Detainee–08's face and beat him for half an hour. Detainee–08 recalled being beaten with a chair until it broke, hit in the chest, kicked, and choked until he lost consciousness. On other occasions Detainee–08 recalled that Corporal Graner would throw his food into the toilet and say "go take it and eat it." Detainee–08's claims of abuse do not involve his interrogator(s) and appear to have been committed by Corporal Graner and Staff Sergeant Frederick, both MPs. Reviewing the interrogation reports, however, suggests a correlation between this abuse and his interrogations. Detainee–08's interrogator for his first four interrogations was Soldier–29, a female, and almost certainly the interrogator he spoke of. Her analyst was Soldier–10. In the first interrogation report, they concluded he was lying and recommended a "fear up" approach if he continued to lie. Following his second interrogation it was recommended Detainee–08 be moved to isolation (the Hard Site) as he continued "to be untruthful." Ten days later, a period roughly correlating with Detainee–08's claim of being without clothes and/or a blanket for nine days before his beating, he was interrogated for a third time. The interrogation report references his placement in "the Hole," a small lightless isolation closet, and the "Mutt and Jeff" interrogation technique being employed. Both techniques as they were used here were abusive and unauthorized. According to the report, the interrogators "let the MPs yell at him" and upon their return, "used a fear down," but "he was still holding back." The following day he was interrogated again and the report annotates "use a direct approach with a reminder of the unpleasantness that occurred the last time he lied." Comparing the interrogation reports with Detainee–08's recollections, it is likely the abuse he describes occurred between his third and fourth interrogations and that his interrogators were aware of the abuse, the "unpleasantness." Sergeant Adams stated that

Soldier–29 and Staff Sergeant Frederick had a close personal relationship and it is plausible she had Corporal Graner and Staff Sergeant Frederick "soften up this detainee" as they have claimed "MI" told them to do on several, unspecified occasions.

INCIDENT NO. 5. In October 2003, Detainee–07 reported alleged multiple incidents of physical abuse while in Abu Ghraib. Detainee–07 was an MI Hold and considered of potentially high value. He was interrogated on 8, 21, and 29 October; 4 and 23 November; and 5 December 2003. Detainee–07's claims of physical abuse (hitting) started on his first day of arrival. He was left naked in his cell for extended periods, cuffed in his cell in stressful positions ("High cuffed"), left with a bag over his head for extended periods, and denied bedding or blankets. Detainee–07 described being made to "bark like a dog, being forced to crawl on his stomach while MPs spit and urinated on him, and being struck causing unconsciousness." On another occasion Detainee–07 was tied to a window in his cell and forced to wear women's underwear on his head. On yet another occasion, Detainee–07 was forced to lie down while MPs jumped onto his back and legs. He was beaten with a broom and a chemical light was broken and poured over his body. Detainee–04 witnessed the abuse with the chem-light. During this abuse a police stick was used to sodomize Detainee–07 and two female MPs were hitting him, throwing a ball at his penis and taking photographs. This investigation surfaced no photographic evidence of the chemical light abuse or sodomy. Detainee–07 also alleged that Civilian–17, MP interpreter, Titan Corp., hit Detainee–07 once, cutting his ear to an extent that required stitches. He told Soldier–25, analyst, B/321 MI Battalion, about this hitting incident during an interrogation. Soldier–25 asked the MPs what had happened to the detainee's ear and was told he had fallen in his cell. Soldier–25 did not report the detainee's abuse. Soldier–25 claimed the detainee's allegation was made in the presence of Civilian–21, analyst/interrogator [employed by contractor CACI International, Inc.], Civilian–21 denied hearing. Two photos taken at 2200 hours, 1 November 2003, depict a detainee with stitches in his ear; however, we could not confirm the photo was Detainee–07. Based on the details provided by the detainee and the close correlation to other known MP abuses, it is highly probable Detainee–07's allegations are true. Soldier–25 failed to report the detainee's allegation of abuse. His statements and available photographs do not point to direct MI involvement. However, MI interest in this detainee, his placement in Tier 1A of the Hard Site and initiation of the abuse once he arrived there combine to create a circumstantial connection to MI (knowledge of or implicit tasking of the MPs to "set conditions") which is difficult to ignore. MI should have been aware of what was being done to this detainee based on the frequency of interrogations and high interest in his intelligence value.

INCIDENT NO. 6. Detainee–10 and Detainee–12 claimed that they and "four Iraqi Generals" were abused upon their arrival at the Hard Site. Detainee–10 was documented in MP records as receiving a 1.5 inch laceration on his chin, the result of his resisting an MP transfer. His injuries are likely those captured in several photographs of an unidentified detainee with a lacerated chin and bloody clothing which were taken on 14 November, a date coinciding with his transfer. Detainee–12 claimed he was slammed to the ground, punched, and forced to crawl naked to his cell with a sandbag over his head. These two detainees as well as the other four (Detainee–20, Detainee–19, Detainee–22, Detainee–21) were all high value Iraqi General Officers or senior members of the Iraqi Intelligence Service. MP logs from the Hard Site indicate they attempted to incite a riot in Camp Vigilant while being transferred to the Hard Site. There is no documentation of what occurred at Camp Vigilant or of detainees receiving injuries. When Detainee–10 was in-processed into the Hard Site, he was resisting and was pushed against the wall. At that point the MPs noticed blood coming from under his hood and they discovered the laceration on his chin. A medical corpsman was immediately called to suture the detainee's chin. These events are all documented, indicating the injury occurred before the detainee's arrival at the Hard Site and that he received prompt medical attention. When, where, and by whom this detainee suffered his injuries could not be determined, nor could an evaluation be made of whether it constituted "reasonable force" in conjunction with a riot. Our interest in this incident stems from MP logs concerning Detainee–10 indicating MI provided direction about his treatment. Corporal Graner wrote an entry indicating he was told by Sergeant First Class Joyner, who was in turn told by Lt. Col. [Steven] Jordan, to "Strip them out and PT them." Whether "strip out" meant to remove clothing or to isolate we couldn't determine. Whether "PT them" meant physical stress or abuse can't be determined. The vagueness of this order could, however, have led to any subsequent abuse. The alleged abuse, injury, and harsh treatment correlating with the detainees' transfer to MI Hold also suggest MI could have provided direction or MP could have been given the perception they should abuse or "soften up detainees"; however, there is no clear proof.

INCIDENT NO. 7. On 4 November 2003, a CIA detainee, Detainee–28, died in custody in Tier 1B. Allegedly, a Navy SEAL Team had captured him during a joint Task Force 121/CIA mission. Detainee–28 was suspected of having been involved in an attack against the International Committee of the Red Cross and had numerous weapons with him at the time of his apprehension. He was reportedly resisting arrest, and a SEAL Team member butt-stroked him on the side of the head to suppress the threat he posed. CIA representatives brought Detainee–28 into Abu Ghraib sometime around 0430 to

0530 without notifying JIDC [Joint Interrogation and Detention Center] Operations, in accordance with a supposed verbal agreement with the CIA. While all the details of Detainee–28's death are still not known (CIA, the Department of Justice, and CID have yet to complete and release the results of their investigations), Specialist Stevanus, an MP on duty at the Hard Site at the time Detainee–28 was brought in, stated that two CIA representatives came in with Detainee–28 and he was placed in a shower room (in Tier 1B). About 30 to 45 minutes later, Specialist Stevanus was summoned to the shower stall, and when he arrived, Detainee–28 appeared to be dead. Specialist Stevanus removed the sandbag which was over Detainee–28's head and checked for the detainee's pulse. He found none. He un-cuffed Detainee–28, called for medical assistance, and notified his chain of command. Lieutenant Colonel Jordan stated that he was informed of the death shortly thereafter, at approximately 0715 hours. Lieutenant Colonel Jordan arrived at the Hard Site and talked to Civilian–03, an Iraqi prison medical doctor, who informed him Detainee–28 was dead. Lieutenant Colonel Jordan stated that Detainee–28 was in the Tier 1B shower stall, face down, handcuffed with his hands behind his back. Lieutenant Colonel Jordan's version of the handcuffs conflicts with Specialist Stevanus's account that he un-cuffed Detainee–28. This incident remains under CID and CIA investigation.

A CIA representative identified only as "Other Agency

Employee–01" was present, along with several MPs and U.S. medical staff. Lieutenant Colonel Jordan recalled that it was "Other Agency Employee–01" who un-cuffed Detainee–28 and the body was turned over. Lieutenant Colonel Jordan stated that he did not see any blood anywhere, except for a small spot where Detainee–28's head was touching the floor. Lieutenant Colonel Jordan notified Colonel Pappas (205 MI Brigade Commander), and "Other Agency Employee–01" said he would notify "Other Agency Employee–02," his CIA supervisor. Once "Other Agency Employee–02" arrived, he stated he would call Washington, and also requested that Detainee–28's body be held in the Hard Site until the following day. The body was placed in a body bag, packed in ice, and stored in the shower area. CID was notified and the body was removed from Abu Ghraib the next day on a litter to make it appear as if Detainee–28 was only ill, thereby not drawing the attention of the Iraqi guards and detainees. The body was transported to the morgue at Baghdad International Airport for an autopsy, which concluded that Detainee–28 died of a blood clot in the head, a likely result of injuries he sustained while resisting apprehension. There is no indication or accusations that MI personnel were involved in this incident except for the removal of the body.

INCIDENT NO. 8. On 20 October 2003, Detainee–03 was allegedly stripped and physically abused for sharpening a toothbrush to make a shank (knife-like weapon). Detainee–03 claimed the toothbrush was not his. An MP log book entry by Staff Sergeant Frederick, 372 MPs, directed Detainee–03 to be stripped in his cell for six days. Detainee–03 claimed he was told his clothing and mattress would be taken away as punishment. The next day he claims he was cuffed to his cell door for several hours. He claims he was taken to a closed room where he had cold water poured on him and his face was forced into someone's urine. Detainee–03 claimed he was then beaten with a broom and spat upon, and a female soldier stood on his legs and pressed a broom against his anus. He described getting his clothes during the day from Sergeant Joyner and having them taken away each night by Corporal Graner for the next three days. Detainee–03 was an MI Hold but was not interrogated between 16 September and 2 November 2003. It is plausible his interrogators would be unaware of the alleged abuse and Detainee–03 made no claim he informed them.

INCIDENT NO. 9. Three photographs taken on 25 October 2003 depicted Private First Class England, 372 MP Company, holding a leash which was wrapped around an unidentified detainee's neck. Present in the photograph is Specialist Ambuhl, who was standing to the side watching. Private First Class England claimed in her initial statement to CID that Corporal Graner had placed the tie-down strap around the detainee's neck and then asked her to pose for the photograph. There is no indication of MI involvement or knowledge of this incident.

INCIDENT NO. 10. Six photographs of Detainee–15 depict him standing on a box with simulated electrical wires attached to his fingers and a hood over his head. These photographs were taken between 2145 and 2315 on 4 November 2003. Detainee–15 described a female making him stand on the box, telling him if he fell off he would be electrocuted, and a "tall black man" as putting the wires on his fingers and penis. From the CID investigation into abuse at Abu Ghraib it was determined Sergeant J. Davis, Specialist Harman, Corporal Graner, and Staff Sergeant Frederick, 372 MP Company, were present during this abuse. Detainee–15 was not an MI Hold and it is unlikely MI had knowledge of this abuse.

INCIDENT NO. 11. Twenty-nine photos taken between 2315 and 0024, on 7 and 8 November 2003, depict seven detainees (Detainee–17, Detainee–16, Detainee–24, Detainee–23, Detainee–26, Detainee–01, Detainee–18), who were physically abused, placed in a pile and forced to masturbate. Present in some of these photographs are Corporal Graner and Specialist Harman. The CID investigation into these abuses identified Staff Sergeant Frederick, Corporal Graner, Sergeant J. Davis, Specialist Ambuhl, Specialist Harman, Specialist Sivits, and Private First Class

England, all MPs, as involved in the abuses which occurred. There is no evidence to support MI personnel involvement in this incident. CID statements from Private First Class England, Sergeant J. Davis, Specialist Sivits, Specialist Wisdom, Specialist Harman, Detainee–17, Detainee–01, and Detainee–16 detail that the detainees were stripped, pushed into a pile, and jumped on by Sergeant J. Davis, Corporal Graner, and Staff Sergeant Frederick. They were photographed at different times by Specialist Harman, Specialist Sivits, and Staff Sergeant Frederick. The detainees were subsequently posed sexually, forced to masturbate, and "ridden like animals." Corporal Graner knocked at least one detainee unconscious, and Staff Sergeant Frederick punched one so hard in the chest that he couldn't breath and a medic was summoned. Staff Sergeant Frederick initiated the masturbation and forced the detainees to hit each other. Private First Class England stated she observed Staff Sergeant Frederick strike a detainee in the chest during these abuses. The detainee had difficulty breathing and a medic, Soldier–01, was summoned. Soldier–01 treated the detainee and while in the Hard Site observed the "human pyramid" of naked detainees with bags over their heads. Soldier–01 failed to report this abuse. These detainees were not MI Holds and MI involvement in this abuse has not been alleged nor is it likely. Soldier–29 reported seeing a screen saver for a computer in the Hard Site that depicted several naked detainees stacked in a "pyramid." She also once observed, unrelated to this incident, Corporal Graner slap a detainee.

She stated that she didn't report the picture of naked detainees to MI because she did not see it again and also did not report the slap because she didn't consider it abuse.

Incident No. 12. A photograph taken circa 27 December 2003, depicts a naked Detainee–14, apparently shot with a shotgun in his buttocks. This photograph could not be tied to a specific incident, detainee, or allegation and MI involvement is indeterminate.

Incident No. 13. Three photographs taken on 29 November 2003, depict an unidentified detainee dressed only in his underwear, standing with each foot on a separate box, and bent over at the waist. This photograph could not be tied to a specific incident, detainee, or allegation and MI involvement is indeterminate.

Incident No. 14. An 18 November 2003 photograph depicts a detainee dressed in a shirt or blanket lying on the floor with a banana inserted into his anus. This as well as several others show the same detainee covered in feces, with his hands encased in sandbags, or tied in foam and between two stretchers. These are all identified as Detainee–25 and were determined by CID investigation to be self-inflicted incidents. Even so, these incidents constitute abuse; a detainee with a known mental condition should not have been provided the banana or photographed. The detainee has a severe mental problem and the restraints depicted in these photographs were allegedly used to prevent the detainee from sodomizing himself and assaulting himself and others with his bodily fluids. He was known for inserting various objects into his rectum and for consuming and throwing his urine and feces. MI had no association with this detainee.

INCIDENT NO. 15. On 26 or 27 November 2003, Soldier–15, 66 MI Group, observed Civilian–11, a CACI contractor, interrogating an Iraqi policeman. During the interrogation, Staff Sergeant Frederick, 372 MP Company, alternated between coming into the cell and standing next to the detainee and standing outside the cell. Civilian–11 would ask the policeman a question stating that if he did not answer, he would bring Staff Sergeant Frederick back into the cell. At one point, Staff Sergeant Frederick put his hand over the policeman's nose, not allowing him to breathe for a few seconds. At another point Staff Sergeant Frederick used a collapsible nightstick to push and possibly twist the policeman's arm, causing pain. When Staff Sergeant Frederick walked out of the cell, he told Soldier–15 he knew ways to do this without leaving marks. Soldier–15 did not report the incident. The interpreter utilized for this interrogation was Civilian–16.

INCIDENT NO. 16. On an unknown date, Sergeant Hernandez, an analyst, observed Civilian–05, a CACI contractor, grab a detainee from the back of a High-Mobility, Multipurpose, Wheeled Vehicle and drop him on the ground. Civilian–05 then dragged the detainee into an interrogation booth. The detainee was handcuffed the entire time. When the detainee tried to get up to his knees, Civilian–05 would force him to fall. Sergeant Hernandez reported the incident to CID but did not report it in MI channels.

INCIDENT NO. 17. A 30 November 2003 MP log entry described an unidentified detainee found in a cell covered in blood. This detainee had assaulted Corporal Graner, 372 MP Company, while they moved him to an isolation cell in Tier 1A. Corporal Graner and Corporal Kamauf subdued the detainee, placed restraints on him and put him in an isolation cell. At approximately 0320 hours, 30 November 2003, after hearing banging on the isolation cell door, the cell was checked and the detainee was found in the cell standing by the door covered in blood. This detainee was not an MI Hold and there is no record of MI association with this incident or detainee.

INCIDENT NO. 18. On approximately 12 or 13 December 2003, Detainee–06 claimed numerous abuse incidents against U.S. soldiers. Detainee–06 was a Syrian foreign fighter and self-proclaimed Jihadist who came to Iraq to kill Coalition troops. Detainee–06 stated the soldiers supposedly retaliated against him when he returned to the Hard Site after being released from the hospital following a shooting incident in which he attempted to kill U.S. soldiers. Detainee–06 had a pistol smuggled in to him by an Iraqi policeman and used that pistol to try to kill U.S. personnel working in the Hard Site on 24 November 2003. An MP returned fire and wounded Detainee–06. Once Detainee–06 ran out of ammunition, he surrendered and was transported to the hospital. Detainee–06 claimed Civilian–21 visited him in the hospital and threatened him with terrible torture upon his return. Detainee–06 claimed that upon his return to the Hard Site, he was subjected to various threats and abuses which included soldiers threatening to torture and kill him, being forced to eat pork and having liquor put in his mouth, having a "very hot" substance put in his nose and on his forehead, having the guards hit his "broken" leg several times with a solid plastic stick, being forced to "curse" his religion, being urinated on, being hung by handcuffs from the cell door for hours, being "smacked" on the back of the head, and "allowing dogs to try to bite" him. This claim was substantiated by a medic, Soldier–20, who was called to treat a detainee (Detainee–06) who had been complaining of pain. When Soldier–20 arrived Detainee–06 was cuffed to the upper bunk so that he could not sit down and Corporal Graner was poking at his wounded legs with an asp, with Detainee–06 crying out in pain. Soldier–20 provided pain medication and departed. He returned the following day to find Detainee–06 again cuffed to the upper bunk and a few days later returned to find him cuffed to the cell door with a dislocated shoulder. Soldier–20 failed to either stop or report this abuse. Detainee–06 also claimed that prior to the shooting incident, which he described as when "I got shot with several bullets" without mentioning that he ever fired a shot, he was threatened "every one or two hours ... with torture and punishment," was subjected to sleep deprivation by standing up "for hours and hours," and had a "black man" tell him he would rape Detainee–06 on two occasions. Although Detainee–06 stated that Corporal Graner led "a number of soldiers" into his cell, he also stated that he had never seen Corporal Graner beat a prisoner. These claims are from a detainee who attempted to kill U.S. service members. While it is likely some soldiers treated Detainee–06 harshly upon his return to the Hard Site, Detainee–06's accusations are potentially the exaggerations of a man who hated Americans.

INCIDENT NO. 19. Sergeant Adams, 470 MI Group, stated that sometime between 4 and 13 December 2003, several weeks after the shooting of "a detainee who had a pistol" (Detainee–06), she heard he was back from the hospital, and she went to check on him because he was one of the MI Holds she interrogated. She found

Detainee–06 without clothes or blanket. His wounds were bleeding and he had a catheter on without a bag. The MPs told her they had no clothes for the detainee. Sergeant Adams ordered the MPs to get the detainee some clothes and went to the medical site to get the doctor on duty. The doctor (Colonel) asked what Sergeant Adams wanted and he was asked if he was aware the detainee still had a catheter on. The Colonel said he was, the Combat Army Surgical Hospital (CASH) had made a mistake, and he couldn't remove it because the CASH was responsible for it. Sergeant Adams told him this was unacceptable, he again refused to remove it and stated the detainee was due to go back to the CASH the following day. Sergeant Adams asked if he had ever heard of the Geneva Conventions, and the Colonel responded "Fine, Sergeant, you do what you have to do. I am going back to bed."

It is apparent from this incident that Detainee–06 did not receive proper medical treatment, clothing or bedding. The "Colonel" has not been identified in this investigation, but efforts continue. Lieutenant Colonel Akerson was chief of the medical team for "security holds" at Abu Ghraib from early October to late December 2003. He treated Detainee–06 following his shooting and upon his return from the hospital. He did not recall such an incident or Detainee–06 having a catheter. It is possible Sergeant Adams was taken to a different doctor that evening. She asked and was told the doctor was a Colonel, not a Lieutenant Colonel, and is confident she can identify the Colonel from a photograph. Lieutenant Colonel Akerson characterized the medical records as being exceptional at Abu Ghraib; however, the records found by this investigation were poor and in most cases non-existent.

INCIDENT NO. 20. During the fall of 2003, a detainee stated that another detainee, named Detainee–09, was stripped, forced to stand on two boxes, had water poured on him and had his genitals hit with a glove. Additionally, the detainee was handcuffed to his cell door for a half day without food or water. The detainee making the statement did not recall the exact date or participants. Later, "Assad" was identified as Detainee–09, who stated that on 5 November 2003 he was stripped naked, beaten, and forced to crawl on the floor. He was forced to stand on a box and was hit in his genitals. The participants in this abuse could not be determined. MI involvement is indeterminate.

INCIDENT NO. 21. Circa October 2003, Civilian–17, an interpreter of the Titan Corporation, observed the following incident: Corporal Graner, 372 MP Company, pushed a detainee, identified as one of the "three stooges" or "three wise men," into a wall, lacerating the detainee's chin. Civilian–17 specifically stated the detainee was pushed into a wall and "busted his chin." A medic, Sergeant Wallin, stated he was summoned to stitch the detainee and treated a 2.5 inch laceration on the detainee's chin requiring 13 stitches. Sergeant Wallin did not know how the detainee was injured. Later that evening, Corporal Graner took photos of the detainee. Corporal Graner was identified in another incident where he stitched an injured detainee in the presence of medics. There is no indication of MI involvement, knowledge, or direction of this abuse.

INCIDENT No. 22. On an unknown date, an interpreter named "Civilian–01" allegedly raped a 15- to 18-year-old male detainee, according to Detainee–05. Detainee–05 heard screaming and climbed to the top of his cell door to see over a sheet covering the door of the cell where the abuse was occurring. Detainee–05 observed Civilian–01, who was wearing a military uniform, raping the detainee. A female soldier was taking pictures. Detainee–05 described Civilian–01 as possibly Egyptian, "not skinny or short," and effeminate. The date and participants of this alleged rape could not be confirmed. No other reporting supports Detainee–05's allegation, nor have photographs of the rape surfaced. A review of all available records could not identify a translator by the name of Civilian–01. Detainee–05's description of the interpreter partially matches Civilian–17, interpreter, Titan Corp. Civilian–17 is a large man, believed by several witnesses to be homosexual, and of Egyptian extraction. Civilian–17 functioned as an interpreter for a Tactical Human Intelligence Team at Abu Ghraib, but routinely provided translation for both MI and MP. CID has an open investigation into this allegation.

INCIDENT NO. 23. On 24 November 2003, a U.S. Army officer, Captain Brinson, MP, allegedly beat and kicked a detainee. This is one of three identified abuses associated with the 24 November shooting. A detainee obtained a pistol from Iraqi police guards, shot an MP and was subsequently shot and wounded. During a subsequent search of the Hard Site and interrogation of detainees, Sergeant Spiker, 229 MP Company, a member of the Abu Ghraib Internal Reaction Force, observed an Army captain dragging an unidentified detainee in a choke hold, throwing him against a wall, and kicking him in the mid-section. Specialist Polak, 229 MP Company, IRF, was also present in the Hard Site and observed the same abuse involving two soldiers and a detainee. The detainee was lying on his stomach with his hands cuffed behind his back and a bag over his head. One soldier stood next to him with the barrel of a rifle pressed against the detainee's head. The other soldier was kneeling next to the detainee punching him in the back with a closed fist. The soldier then stood up and kicked the detainee several times. The soldier inflicting the beating was described as a white male with close cropped blond hair. Specialist Polak saw this soldier a few days later in full uniform, identifying him as a Captain, but could not see his name. Both Specialist Polak and Sergeant Spiker reported this abuse to their supervisors, Sergeant First Class Plude and First Lieutenant Sutton, 372 MP Company. Photos of company grade officers at Abu Ghraib during this time were obtained and shown to Specialist Polak and Sergeant Spiker, who positively identified the "Captain" as Captain Brinson. This incident was investigated by CID and the assault was determined to be unfounded; a staged event to protect the fact the detainee was a cooperative MP Source.

INCIDENT NO. 24. A photograph created circa early December 2003 depicts an unidentified detainee being interrogated by Civilian–11, CACI, interrogator, and Civilian–16, Titan, linguist. The detainee is squatting on a chair, which is an unauthorized stress position. Having the detainee on a chair, which is a potentially unsafe situation, and photographing the detainee are violations of the Interrogation and Counter-Resistance Policies.

INCIDENTS OF DETAINEE
ABUSE USING DOGS

Abusing detainees with dogs started almost immediately after the dogs arrived at Abu Ghraib on 20 November 2003. By that date, abuse of detainees was already occurring and the addition of dogs was just one more abuse device. Dog teams were brought to Abu Ghraib as a result of recommendations from Maj. Gen. G. Miller's assessment team from Joint Task Force Guantanamo. Maj. Gen. G. Miller recommended dogs as beneficial for detainee custody and control issues, especially in instances where there were large numbers of detainees and few guards to help reduce the risk of detainee demonstrations or acts of violence, as at Abu Ghraib. Maj. Gen. G. Miller never recommended, nor were dogs used for, interrogations at Guantanamo. The dog teams were requested by Colonel Pappas, Commander, 205 MI Brigade. Colonel Pappas never understood the intent as described by Maj. Gen. G. Miller. Interrogations at Abu Ghraib were also influenced by several documents that spoke of exploiting the Arab fear of dogs: a 24 January 2003 "CJTF 180 Interrogation Techniques," an 11 October 2002 Joint Task Force 170 "Counter-Resistance Strategies," and a 14 September 2003 CJTF–7 Interrogation and Counter-Resistance Policy (ICRP). Once the dogs arrived, there was controversy over who "owned" the dogs. It was ultimately decided that the dogs would be attached to the Internal Reaction Force. The use of dogs in interrogations to "fear up" detainees was generally unquestioned and stems in part from the interrogation techniques and counter-resistance policy distributed from CJTF 180, Joint Task Force 170 and CJTF–7. It is likely the confusion about using dogs partially stems from the initial request for dog teams by MI, not MPs, and their presence being associated with Maj. Gen. G. Miller's visit. Most military intelligence personnel believed that the use of dogs in interrogations was a "non-standard" technique which required approval, and most also believed that approval rested with Colonel Pappas. Colonel Pappas also believed, incorrectly, that he had such authority delegated to him from Lt. Gen. [Ricardo] Sanchez. Colonel Pappas's belief likely stemmed in part from the changing ICRP. The initial policy was published on 14 September 2003 and allowed the use of dogs subject to approval by Lieutenant General Sanchez. On 12 October 2003, these were amended to eliminate several techniques due to objections by the U.S. Central Command. After the 12 October 2003 amendment, the ICRP safeguards allowed that dogs present at interrogations were to be muzzled and under the control of a handler. Colonel Pappas did not recall how he got the authority to employ dogs; just that he had it.

Sergeant First Class Plude stated the two Army dog teams never joined the Navy teams as part of the IRF and remained separate and under the direct control of Major Dinenna, S3, 320 MP Battalion. These teams were involved in all documented detainee abuse involving dogs, both MP and MI directed. The Navy dog teams were properly employed because of good training, excellent leadership, personal moral character, and professionalism exhibited by the Navy Dog Handlers, Master-at-Arms First Class Kimbro, Master-at-Arms First Class Clark, and Master-at-Arms Second Class Pankratz, and IRF personnel. The Army teams apparently agreed to be used in abusive situations by both MPs and MI in contravention to their doctrine, training, and values. In an atmosphere of permissiveness and absence of oversight or leadership, the Army dog teams became involved in several incidents of abuse over the following weeks.

INCIDENT No. 25. The first documented incident of abuse with dogs occurred on 24 November 2003, just four days after the dog teams arrived. An Iraqi detainee was smuggled a pistol by an Iraqi Police Guard. While attempting to confiscate the weapon, an MP was shot and the detainee was subsequently shot and wounded. Following the shooting, Lieutenant Colonel Jordan ordered several interrogators to the Hard Site to screen 11 Iraqi police who were detained following the shooting. The situation at the Hard Site was described by many as "chaos," and no one really appeared to be in charge. The perception was that Lieutenant General Sanchez had removed all restrictions that night because of the situation; however, that was not true. No one is able to pin down how that perception was created. A Navy dog team entered the Hard Site and was instructed to search for additional weapons and explosives. The dogs searched the cells, no explosives were detected and the Navy dog team eventually completed their mission and left. Shortly thereafter, Master-at-Arms First Class Kimbro, USN, was recalled when someone "needed" a dog. Master-at-Arms First Class Kimbro went to the top floor of Tier 1B, rather than the MI Hold area of Tier 1A. As he and his dog approached a cell door, he heard yelling and screaming and his dog became agitated. Inside the cell were Civilian–11 (CACI contract interrogator), a second unidentified male in civilian clothes who appeared to be an interrogator and Civilian–16 (female contract interpreter), all of whom were yelling at a detainee squatting in the back right corner. Master-at-Arms First Class Kimbro's dog was barking a lot with all the yelling and commotion. The dog lunged and Master-at-Arms First Class Kimbro struggled to regain control of it. At that point, one of the men said words to the effect "You see that dog there, if you don't tell me what I want to know, I'm gonna get that dog on you!" The three began to step out of the cell, leaving the detainee inside, and Master-at-Arms First Class Kimbro backed up to allow them to exit, but there was not much room on the tier. After they exited, the dog lunged and pulled Master-at-Arms First Class Kimbro just inside the cell. He quickly regained control of his dog, and exited the cell. As Civilian–11, Civilian–16, and the other interrogator re-entered the cell, Master-at-Arms First Class Kimbro's dog grabbed Civilian–16's forearm in its mouth. It apparently did not bite through her clothes or skin and Civilian–16 stated the dog did not bite her. Realizing he had not been called for an explosives search, Master-at-Arms First Class Kimbro departed the area with his dog and as he got to the bottom of the tier stairs, he heard someone calling for the dog again, but he did not return. No record of this interrogation exists, as was the case for the interrogations of

Iraqi police in the hours and days following the shooting incident. The use of dogs in the manner directed by Civilian–11 was clearly abusive and unauthorized.

Even with all the apparent confusion over roles, responsibilities and authorities, there were early indications that MP and MI personnel knew the use of dog teams in interrogations was abusive. Following this 24 November 2003 incident the three Navy dog teams concluded that some interrogators might attempt to misuse Navy dogs to support their interrogations. For all subsequent requests they inquired what the specific purpose of the dog was and when told "for interrogation" they explained that Navy dogs were not intended for interrogations and the request would not be fulfilled. Over the next few weeks, the Navy dog teams received about eight similar calls, none of which were fulfilled. In the later part of December 2003, Colonel Pappas summoned Master-at-Arms First Class Kimbro and wanted to know what the Navy dogs' capabilities were. Master-at-Arms First Class Kimbro explained Navy dog capabilities and provided the Navy Dog Use SOP. Colonel Pappas never asked if they could be used in interrogations, and following that meeting the Navy dog teams received no additional requests to support interrogations.

INCIDENT NO. 26. On or about 8 January 2004, Soldier–17 was conducting an interrogation of a Baath Party General Officer in the shower area of Tier 1B of the

Hard Site. Tier 1B was the area of the Hard Site dedicated to female and juvenile detainees. Although Tier 1B was not the normal location for interrogations, due to a space shortage in Tier 1A, Soldier–17 was using this area. Soldier–17 witnessed an MP guard and an MP dog handler, whom Soldier–17 later identified from photographs as Soldier–27, enter Tier 1B with Soldier–27's black dog. The dog was on a leash, but was not muzzled. The MP guard and MP dog handler opened a cell in which two juveniles, one known as "Casper," were housed. Soldier–27 allowed the dog to enter the cell and "go nuts on the kids," barking at and scaring them. The juveniles were screaming and the smaller one tried to hide behind "Casper." Soldier–27 allowed the dog to get within about one foot of the juveniles. Afterward, Soldier–17 overheard Soldier–27 say that he had a competition with another handler (likely Soldier–08, the only other Army dog handler) to see if they could scare detainees to the point that they would defecate. He mentioned that they had already made some detainees urinate, so they appeared to be raising the competition. This incident has no direct MI involvement; however, Soldier–17 failed to properly report what he observed. He stated that he went to bed and forgot the incident until asked about misuse of dogs during this investigation.

INCIDENT NO. 27. On 12 December 2003, an MI Hold detainee named Detainee–11 was recommended by MI

(Soldier–17) for an extended stay in the Hard Site because he appeared to be mentally unstable. He was bitten by a dog in the Hard Site, but at the time he was not undergoing an interrogation and no MI personnel were present. Detainee–11 told Soldier–17 that a dog had bitten him and Soldier–17 saw dog bite marks on Detainee–11's thigh. Soldier–08, who was the dog handler of the dog that bit Detainee–11, stated that in December 2003 his dog bit a detainee and he believed that MPs were the only personnel around when the incident occurred, but he declined to make further statements regarding this incident to either the inquiry by Major General Taguba or to this inquiry. Soldier–27, another Army dog handler, also stated that Soldier–08's dog had bitten someone, but did not provide further information. This incident was captured on digital photograph 0178/CG LAPS and appears to be the result of MP harassment and amusement; no MI involvement is suspected.

INCIDENT NO. 28. In an apparent MI-directed use of dogs, circa 18 December 2003, a photograph depicts a Syrian detainee (Detainee–14) kneeling on the floor with his hands bound behind his back. Detainee–14 was a "high value" detainee who had arrived at Abu Ghraib in December 2003 from a Navy ship. Detainee–14 was suspected to be involved with Al-Qaeda. Military working dog handler Soldier–27 is standing in front of

Detainee–14 with his black dog a few feet from Detainee–14's face. The dog is leashed, but not muzzled. Sergeant Eckroth was Detainee–14's interrogator from 18 to 21 December 2003, and Civilian–21, CACI contract interrogator, assumed the lead after Sergeant Eckroth departed Abu Ghraib on 22 December 2003. Sergeant Eckroth identified Detainee–14 as his detainee when shown a photo of the incident. Civilian–21 claimed to know nothing about this incident; however, in December 2003 he related to Sergeant Eckroth he was told by MPs that Detainee–14's bedding had been ripped apart by dogs. Civilian–21 was characterized by Soldier–25 as having a close relationship with the MPs, and she was told by Sergeant Frederick about dogs being used when Civilian–21 was there. It is highly plausible that Civilian–21 used dogs without authorization and directed the abuse in this incident as well as others related to this detainee.

INCIDENT No. 29. On or about 14–15 December 2003, dogs were used in an interrogation. Specialist Aston, who was the section chief of the special projects team, stated that on 14 December, one of his interrogation teams requested the use of dogs for a detainee captured in conjunction with the capture of Saddam Hussein on 13 December 2003. Specialist Aston verbally requested the use of dogs from Colonel Pappas, and Colonel Pappas stated that he would call higher to request permission.

This is contrary to Colonel Pappas's statement that he was given authority to use dogs as long as they were muzzled. About one hour later, Specialist Aston received approval. Specialist Aston stated that he was standing to the side of the dog handler the entire time the dog was used in the interrogation. The dog never hurt anyone and was always muzzled, about five feet away from the detainee.

INCIDENT NO. 30. On another occasion, Soldier–26, an MI soldier assigned to the S2, 320 MP Battalion, was present during an interrogation of a detainee and was told the detainee was suspected to have Al-Qaeda affiliations. Dogs were requested and approved about three days later. Soldier–26 didn't know if the dog had to be muzzled or not, likely telling the dog handler to un-muzzle the dog, in contravention to CJTF–7 policy. The interrogators were Civilian–20, CACI, and Civilian–21 (CACI). Soldier–14, Operations Officer, Interrogation and Control Element, stated that Civilian–21 used a dog during one of his interrogations and this is likely that occasion. According to Soldier–14, Civilian–21 had the dog handler maintain control of the dog and did not make any threatening reference to the dog, but apparently "felt just the presence of the dog would be unsettling to the detainee." Soldier–14 did not know who approved the procedure, but was verbally notified by Soldier–23, who supposedly received the approval from

Colonel Pappas. Civilian–21 claimed he once requested to use dogs, but it was not approved. Based on the evidence, Civilian–21 was deceitful in his statement.

Incident No. 31. In a 14–15 December 2003 interrogation, military working dogs were used but were deemed ineffective because the detainee had little to no response to them. Civilian–11, Soldier–05 and Soldier–12, who all participated in the interrogation, believed they had authority to use the dogs from Colonel Pappas or from Lieutenant General Sanchez; however, no documentation was found showing CJTF–7 approval to use dogs in interrogations. It is probable that approval was granted by Colonel Pappas without such authority. Lieutenant General Sanchez stated he never approved use of dogs.

Incident No. 32. In yet another instance, Soldier–25, an interrogator, stated that when she and Soldier–15 were interrogating a female detainee in the Hard Site, they heard a dog barking. The female detainee was frightened by dogs, and Soldier–25 and Soldier–15 returned her to her cell. Soldier–25 went to see what was happening with the dog barking and saw a detainee in his underwear on a mattress on the floor of Tier 1A with a dog standing over him. Civilian–21 was upstairs giving directions to Staff Sergeant Frederick (372 MP Company), telling him to "take him back home." Soldier–25 opined it was "common knowledge that Civilian–21 used dogs while he was on special projects, working directly for Colonel Pappas after the capture of Saddam on 13 December 2003." Soldier–25 could not identify anyone else specifically who knew of this "common knowledge." It appeared Civilian–21 was encouraging and even directing the MP abuse with dogs; likely a "softening up" technique for future interrogations. The detainee was one of Civilian–21's. Soldier–25 did not see an interpreter in the area, so it is unlikely that Civilian–21 was actually doing an interrogation.

Soldier–25 stated that Staff Sergeant Frederick would come into her office every other day or so and tell her about dogs being used while Civilian–21 was present. Staff Sergeant Frederick and other MPs used to refer to "doggy dance" sessions. Soldier–25 did not specify what "doggy dance" was, but the obvious implication is that it referred to an unauthorized use of dogs to intimidate detainees.

INCIDENTS OF DETAINEE ABUSE USING HUMILIATION

Removal of clothing was not a technique developed at Abu Ghraib, but rather a technique which was imported and can be traced through Afghanistan and Guantanamo. The 1987 version of Field Manual 34–52, Interrogation, talked about "controlling all aspects of the interrogation to include ... clothing given to the source," while the current 1992 version does not. The 1987 version was, however, cited as the primary reference for CJTF–7 in Iraq, even as late as 9 June 2004. The removal of clothing for both MI and MP objectives was authorized, approved, and employed in Afghanistan and Guantanamo. At Guantanamo, the Joint Task Force 170 "Counter-Resistance Strategy," documented on 11 October 2002, permitted the removal of clothing, approved by the interrogation officer-in-charge, as an incentive in detention operations and interrogations. The Secretary of Defense granted this authority on 2 December 2002, but it was rescinded six weeks later in January 2003. This technique also surfaced in Afghanistan. The CJTF–180 "Interrogation Techniques," documented on 24 January 2003, highlighted that deprivation of clothing had not historically been included in battlefield interrogations. However, it went on to recommend clothing removal as an effective technique that could potentially raise objections as being degrading or inhumane, but for which no specific written legal prohibition existed. As interrogation operations in Iraq began to take form, it was often the same personnel who had operated and deployed in other theaters and in support of the Global War on Terror who were called upon to establish and conduct interrogation operations in Abu Ghraib. The lines of authority and the prior legal opinions blurred. Soldiers simply carried forward the use of nudity into the Iraqi theater of operations.

Removal of clothing is not a doctrinal or authorized

interrogation technique but appears to have been directed and employed at various levels within MI as an "ego down" technique. It was also employed by MPs as a "control" mechanism. Individual observation and/or understanding of the use and approval of clothing removal varied in each interview conducted by this investigation. Lieutenant Colonel Jordan was knowledgeable of naked detainees and removal of their clothing. He denied ordering it and blamed it on the MPs. Captain Wood and Soldier–14 claimed not to have observed nudity or approved clothing removal. Multiple MPs, interrogators, analysts, and interpreters observed nudity and/or employed clothing removal as an incentive, while an equal number didn't. It is apparent from this investigation that removal of clothing was employed routinely and with the belief it was not abuse. Soldier–03, Guantanamo Tiger Team, believed that removal of clothing as an "ego down" technique could be employed. He thought, mistakenly, that Guantanamo still had that authority. Nudity of detainees throughout the Hard Site was common enough that even during a Red Cross visit they noted several detainees without clothing, and Captain Reese, 372 MP Company, stated upon his initial arrival at Abu Ghraib, "There's a lot of nude people here." Some of the nudity was attributed to a lack of clothing and uniforms for the detainees; however, even in these cases we could not determine what happened to the detainee's original clothing. It was routine practice to strip search detainees before their movement to the Hard

Site. The use of clothing as an incentive (nudity) is significant in that it likely contributed to an escalating "dehumanization" of the detainees and set the stage for additional and more severe abuses to occur.

INCIDENT NO. 33. There is also ample evidence of detainees being forced to wear women's underwear, sometimes on their heads. These cases appear to be a form of humiliation, either for MP control or MI "ego down." Detainee–07 and Detainee–05 both claimed they were stripped of their clothing and forced to wear women's underwear on their heads. Civilian–15 (CACI) and Civilian–19 (CACI), a CJTF–7 analyst, alleged Civilian–21 bragged and laughed about shaving a detainee and forcing him to wear red women's underwear. Several photographs include unidentified detainees with underwear on their heads. Such photos show abuse and constitute sexual humiliation of detainees.

INCIDENT NO. 34. On 16 September 2003, MI directed the removal of a detainee's clothing. This is the earliest incident we identified at Abu Ghraib. An MP log indicated a detainee "was stripped down per MI and he is neked [sic] and standing tall in his cell." The following day his interrogators, Specialist Webster and Staff Sergeant Clinscales, arrived at the detainee's cell, and he was unclothed. They were both surprised. An MP asked

Staff Sergeant Clinscales, a female, to stand to the side while the detainee dressed, and the detainee appeared to have his clothing in his cell. Staff Sergeant Clinscales was told by the MP the detainee had voluntarily removed his clothing as a protest and, in the subsequent interrogation, the detainee did not claim any abuse or the forcible removal of his clothing. It does not appear the detainee was stripped at the interrogator's direction, but someone in MI most likely directed it. Specialist Webster and Soldier–25 provided statements where they opined Specialist Claus, in charge of in-processing MI Holds, may have directed removal of detainee clothing on this and other occasions. Specialist Claus denies ever giving such orders.

INCIDENT NO. 35. On 19 September 2003, an interrogation "Tiger Team" consisting of Soldier–16, Soldier–07, and a civilian contract interpreter identified only as "Maher" (female), conducted a late night/early morning interrogation of a 17-year-old Syrian foreign fighter. Soldier–16 was the lead interrogator. Soldier–07 was told by Soldier–16 that the detainee they were about to interrogate was naked. Soldier–07 was unsure if Soldier–16 was simply passing along that fact or had directed the MPs to strip the detainee. The detainee had fashioned an empty "Meals-Ready-to-Eat" bag to cover his genital area. Soldier–07 couldn't recall who ordered the detainee to raise his hands to his sides, but when he did, the bag fell to the floor, exposing him to Soldier–07 and the two female interrogation team members. Soldier–16 used a direct interrogation approach with the incentive of getting back clothing, and the use of stress positions.

There is no record of an Interrogation Plan or any approval documents which would authorize these techniques. The fact these techniques were documented in the Interrogation Report suggests, however, that the interrogators believed they had the authority to use clothing as an incentive, as well as stress positions, and were not attempting to hide their use. Stress positions were permissible with Commander, CJTF–7 approval at that time. It is probable that use of nudity was sanctioned at some level within the chain-of-command. If not, lack of leadership and oversight permitted the nudity to occur. Having a detainee raise his hands to expose himself in front of two females is humiliation and therefore violates the Geneva Conventions.

INCIDENT NO. 36. In early October 2003, Soldier–19 was conducting an interrogation and ordered a detainee to roll his orange jumpsuit down to his waist, insinuating to the detainee that he would be further stripped if he did not cooperate. Soldier–19's interpreter put up his hand, looked away, said that he was not comfortable with the situation, and exited the interrogation booth. Soldier–19 was then forced to stop the interrogation due to lack of language support. Soldier–11, an analyst from a visiting Joint Task Force Guantanamo Tiger Team, witnessed this incident through the booth's observation window and brought it to the attention of Soldier–16, who was Soldier–19's Team Chief and first line supervisor. Soldier–16 responded that Soldier–19 knew what he was doing and did not take any action regarding the matter. Soldier–11 reported the same information to Soldier–28, his Joint Task Force Guantanamo Tiger Team Chief, who, according to Soldier–11, said he would "take care of it." Soldier–28 recalled a conversation with Soldier–11 concerning an interpreter walking out of an interrogation due to a "cultural difference," but could not remember the incident. This incident has four abuse components: the actual unauthorized stripping of a detainee by Soldier–19, the failure of Soldier–10 to report the incident he witnessed, the failure of Soldier–16 to take corrective action, reporting the incident up the chain of command, and the failure of Soldier–28 to report.

INCIDENT No. 37. A photograph taken on 17 October 2003 depicts a naked detainee chained to his cell door with a hood on his head. Several other photographs taken on 18 October 2003 depict a hooded detainee cuffed to his cell door. Additional photographs on 19 October 2003 depict a detainee cuffed to his bed with underwear on his head. A review of available documents could not tie these photos to a specific incident, detainee or allegation, but these photos reinforce the reality that humiliation and nudity were being employed routinely enough that photo opportunities occurred on three successive days. MI involvement in these apparent abuses cannot be confirmed.

INCIDENT NO. 38. Eleven photographs of two female detainees arrested for suspected prostitution were obtained. Identified in these photographs are Specialist Harman and Corporal Graner, both MPs. In some of these photos, a criminal detainee housed in the Hard Site was shown lifting her shirt with both her breasts exposed. There is no evidence to confirm if these acts were consensual or coerced; however in either case sexual exploitation of a person in U.S. custody constitutes abuse. There does not appear to be any direct MI involvement in either of the two incidents above.

INCIDENT NO. 39. On 16 November 2003, Soldier–29 decided to strip a detainee in response to what she believed was uncooperative and physically recalcitrant behavior. She had submitted an Interrogation Plan in which she planned to use the "Pride and Ego Down," technique but did not specify that she would strip the detainee as part of that approach. Soldier–29 felt the detainee was "arrogant," and when she and her analyst, Soldier–10, "placed him against the wall" the detainee pushed Soldier–10. Soldier–29 warned if he touched Soldier–10 again, she would have him remove his shoes. A bizarre tit-for-tat scenario then ensued where Soldier–29 would warn the detainee about touching Soldier–10, the detainee would "touch" Soldier–10, and then had his shirt, blanket, and finally his pants removed. At this point, Soldier–29 concluded that the detainee was "completely uncooperative" and terminated the interrogation. While nudity seemed to be acceptable, Soldier–29 went further than most when she walked the semi-naked detainee across the camp. Sergeant Adams, Soldier–29's supervisor, commented that walking a semi-naked detainee across the camp could have caused a riot. Civilian–21, a CACI contract interrogator, witnessed Soldier–29 and Soldier–10 escorting the scantily clad detainee from the Hard Site back to Camp Vigilant, wearing only his underwear and carrying his blanket. Civilian–21 notified Sergeant Adams, who was Soldier–29's section chief, who in turn notified Captain Wood, the Interrogation and Control Element's officer in charge. Sergeant Adams immediately called Soldier–29 and Soldier–10 into her office, counseled them, and removed them from interrogation duties.

The incident was relatively well known among Joint Interrogation and Detention Center personnel and appeared in several statements as second hand information when interviewees were asked if they knew of detainee abuse. Lieutenant Colonel Jordan temporarily removed Soldier–29 and Soldier–10 from interrogation duties. Colonel Pappas left the issue for Lieutenant Colonel Jordan to handle. Colonel Pappas should have taken sterner action such as an Article 15, UCMJ. His failure to do so did not send a strong enough message to the rest of the Joint Interrogation and Detention Center that abuse would not be tolerated. Captain Wood had recommended to Lieutenant Colonel Jordan that Soldier–29 receive an Article 15 and Sergeant First Class Johnson, the interrogation non-commissioned officer in charge, recommended she be turned over to her parent unit for the noncompliance.

INCIDENT NO. 40. On 24 November 2003, there was a shooting of a detainee at Abu Ghraib in Tier 1A. Detainee–06, had obtained a pistol. While the MPs attempted to confiscate the weapon, an MP and Detainee–06 were shot. It was alleged that an Iraqi Police Guard had smuggled the pistol to Detainee–06 and in the aftermath of the shooting 43 Iraqi police were screened and 11 subsequently detained and interrogated. All but three were released following intense questioning. A fourth did not report for work the next day and is still at large. The Iraqi guard detainees admitted smuggling the weapons into the facility, hiding them in an inner tube of a tire, and several of the Iraqi guards were identified as Fedayeen trainers and members. During the interrogations of the Iraqi police, harsh and unauthorized techniques were employed, including the use of dogs, discussed earlier in this report, and removal of clothing.

Once detained, the police were strip-searched, which was a reasonable precaution considering the threat of contraband or weapons. Following such search, however, the police were not returned their clothes before being interrogated. This is an act of humiliation and was unauthorized. It was the understanding that evening that Lieutenant General Sanchez and Colonel Pappas had authorized all measures to identify those involved; however, that should not have been construed to include abuse. Lieutenant Colonel Jordan was the senior officer present at the interrogations and is responsible for the harsh and humiliating treatment of the police.

INCIDENT NO. 41. On 4 December 2003, documentation in the MP Logs indicated that MI leadership was aware of clothing removal. An entry indicated "Spoke with Lieutenant Colonel Jordan (205 MI Brigade) about MI Holds in Tier 1A/B. He stated he would clear up with MI and let MPs run Tiers 1A/B as far as what inmate gets [clothes]." Additionally, in his statement, Lieutenant Colonel Phillabaum claims he asked Lieutenant Colonel Jordan what the situation was with naked detainees, and Lieutenant Colonel Jordan responded with, "It was an interrogation technique." Whether this supports allegations of MI involvement in the clothing and stripping of detainees is uncertain, but it does show that MI at least knew of the practice and was willing to defer decisions to the MPs. Such vague guidance, if later combined with an implied tasking from MI, or perceived tasking by MP, potentially contributed to the subsequent abuse.

INCIDENTS OF DETAINEE ABUSE USING ISOLATION

Isolation is a valid interrogation technique which required approval by the CJTF–7 Commander. We identified documentation of four instances where isolation was approved by Lieutenant General Sanchez. Lieutenant General Sanchez stated he had approved 25 instances of isolation. This investigation, however, found numerous incidents of chronic confusion by both MI and MPs at all levels of command, up through CJTF–7, between the definitions of "isolation" and "segregation." Since these terms were commonly interchanged, we conclude segregation was used far more often than isolation. Segregation is a valid procedure to limit collaboration between detainees. This is what was employed most often in Tier 1A (putting a detainee in a cell by himself instead of in a communal cell, as was common outside the Hard Site) and was sometimes incorrectly referred to as "isolation." Tier 1A did have isolation cells with solid doors which could be closed as well as a small room (closet) which was referred to as the isolation "Hole." Use of these rooms should have been closely controlled and monitored by MI and MP leaders. They were not, however, which subjected the detainees to excessive cold in the winter and heat in the summer. There was obviously poor air quality, no monitoring of time limits, no frequent checks on the physical condition of the detainee, and no medical screening, all of which added up to detainee abuse. A review of interrogation reports identified ten references to "putting people in the Hole," "taking them out of the Hole," or consideration of isolation. These occurred between 15 September 2003 and 3 January 2004.

INCIDENT NO. 42. On 15 September 2003, at 2150 hours, unidentified MI personnel, using the initials CKD, directed the use of isolation on an unidentified detainee. The detainee in cell No. 9 was directed to leave his outer cell door open for ventilation and was directed to be taken off the light schedule. The identification of CKD, the MI personnel, or the detainee could not be determined. This information originated from the prison log entry and confirms the use of isolation and sensory deprivation as interrogation techniques.

INCIDENT NO. 43. In early October 2003, Soldier–11 was interrogating an unidentified detainee with Soldier–19, an interrogator, and an unidentified contract interpreter. About an hour and 45 minutes into the interrogation, Soldier–19 turned to Soldier–11 and asked if he thought they should place the detainee in solitary confinement for a few hours, apparently because the detainee was not cooperating or answering questions. Soldier–11 expressed his misgivings about the tactic, but deferred to Soldier–19 as the interrogator. About 15 minutes later, Soldier–19 stopped the interrogation, departed the booth, and returned about five minutes later with an MP, Staff Sergeant Frederick. Staff Sergeant Frederick jammed a bag over the detainee's head, grabbed the handcuffs restraining him and said something like "come with me piggy," as he led the detainee to solitary confinement in the Hard Site, Tier 1A of Abu Ghraib.

About half an hour later, Soldier–19 and Soldier–11 went to the Hard Site without their interpreter, although he was available if needed. When they arrived at the detainee's cell, they found him lying on the floor, completely naked except for a hood that covered his head from his upper lip, whimpering, but there were no bruises or marks on him. Staff Sergeant Frederick then met Soldier–19 and Soldier–11 at the cell door. He started yelling at the detainee, "You've been moving little piggy, you know you shouldn't move," or words to that effect, and yanked the hood back down over the detainee's head. Soldier–19 and Soldier–11 instructed other MPs to clothe the detainee, which they did. Soldier–11 then asked Soldier–19 if he knew the MPs were going to strip the detainee, and Soldier–19 said that he did not. After the detainee was clothed, both Soldier–19 and Soldier–11 escorted him to the general population and released him without interrogating him again. Staff Sergeant Frederick made the statement, "I want to thank you guys, because up until a week or two ago, I was a good Christian." Soldier–11 is uncertain under what context Staff Sergeant Frederick made this statement. Soldier–11 noted that neither the isolation technique, nor the "stripping incident" in the cell, was in any "interrogator notes" or "interrogation plan."

More than likely, Soldier–19 knew what Staff Sergeant Frederick was going to do. Given that the order for isolation appeared to be a spontaneous reaction to the detainee's recalcitrance and not part of an orchestrated Interrogation Plan; that the "isolation" lasted only approximately half an hour; that Soldier–19 chose to re-contact the detainee without an interpreter present; and that Soldier–19 was present with Staff Sergeant Frederick at another incident of detainee abuse, it is possible that Soldier–19 had a prearranged agreement with Staff Sergeant Frederick to "soften up" uncooperative detainees and directed Staff Sergeant Frederick to strip the detainee in isolation as punishment for being uncooperative, thus providing the detainee an incentive to cooperate during the next interrogation. We believe, at a minimum, Soldier–19 knew or at least suspected this type of treatment would take place even without specific instructions.

INCIDENT(S) NO. 44. On 13 November 2003, Soldier–29 and Soldier–10, MI interrogators, noted that a detainee was unhappy with his stay in isolation and visits to the hole.

On 11, 13, and 14 November 2003, MI interrogators Soldier–04, Soldier–09, Soldier–02, and Soldier–23 noted that a detainee was "walked and put in the Hole," "pulled out of extreme segregation," "did not seem to be bothered to return to the Hole," "Kept in the Hole for a long time unless he started to talk," and "was in good spirits even after three days in the Hole."

A 5 November 2003 interrogation report indicates in the recommendations/future approaches paragraph: "Detainee has been recommended for the hole in ISO [isolation]. Detainee should be treated harshly because friendly treatment has not been productive and because Colonel Pappas wants fast resolution, or he will turn the detainee over to someone other than the 205th [MI]."

On 12 November 2003, MI interrogators Soldier–18 and Soldier–13 noted that a detainee "feared the isolation Hole, and it made him upset, but not enough to break."

On 29 November 2003, MI interrogators Soldier–18 and Soldier–06 told a detainee that "he would go into the Hole if he didn't start cooperating."

On 8 December 2003, unidentified interrogators told a detainee that he was "recommended for movement to ISO and the Hole—he was told his sun [sunlight] would be taken away, so he better enjoy it now."

These incidents all indicate the routine and repetitive use of total isolation and light deprivation. Documentation of this technique in the interrogation reports implies those employing it thought it was authorized. The manner in which it was applied is a violation of the Geneva Conventions, CJTF–7 policy, and Army policy.

Several alleged abuses were investigated and found to be unsubstantiated. Others turned out to be no more than general rumor or fabrication. This investigation established a threshold below which information on alleged or potential abuse was not included in this report. Fragmentary or difficult to understand allegations or information at times defied our ability to investigate further. One such example is contained in a statement from an alleged abuse victim, Detainee–13, who claimed he was always treated well at Abu Ghraib but was abused earlier by his captors. He potentially contradicts that claim by stating his head was hit into a wall. The detainee appears confused concerning the times and locations at which he was abused. Several incidents involved numerous victims and/or occurred during a single "event," such as the Iraqi police interrogations on 24 November 2003. One example receiving some visibility was a report by Soldier–22, who overheard a conversation in the "chow hall" between Specialist Mitchell and his unidentified "friends." Specialist Mitchell was alleged to have said: "MPs were using detainees as practice dummies. They would hit the detainees as practice shots. They would apply strikes to their necks and knock them out. One detainee was so scared; the MPs held his head and told him everything would be alright, and then they would strike him. The detainees would plead for mercy and the MPs thought it was all funny." Specialist Mitchell was interviewed and denied having knowledge of any abuse. He admitted that he and his friends would joke about noises they heard in the Hard Site and say things such as "the MPs are doing their thing." Specialist Mitchell never thought anyone would take him seriously. Several associates of Specialist Mitchell were interviewed (Specialist Griffin, Soldier–12, Private Heidenreich). All claimed their discussions with Specialist Mitchell were just rumor, and they didn't think anyone would take him seriously or construe he had personal knowledge of abuse. Specialist Mitchell's duties also make it unlikely he would have witnessed any abuse. He arrived at Abu Ghraib as an analyst, working the day shift, in late November 2003. Shortly after his arrival, the 24 November "shooting incident" occurred, and the following day he was moved to Camp Victory for three weeks. Upon his return, he was transferred to guard duty at Camp Wood and Camp Steel and never returned to the Hard Site. This alleged abuse is likely an individual's boastful exaggeration of a rumor which was rampant throughout Abu Ghraib, nothing more.

Appendix A: Units Involved from Guantanamo, Afghanistan, Iraq

To study how interrogation policies evolved, the Abu Ghraib investigators focused on the links among units from the three main military arenas in the war on terrorism.

Guantanamo

United States Southern Command: One of nine Unified Combatant Commands with operational control of U.S. military forces. Area of responsibility includes Guantanamo Bay, Cuba. Commander: Gen. James Hill.

Joint Task Force 160: Initially responsible for detention operations at Guantanamo, merged in Joint Task Force Guantanamo on November 4, 2002.

Joint Task Force 170: Initially responsible for interrogation operations at Guantanamo, merged in Joint Task Force Guantanamo on November 4, 2002.

Joint Task Force Guantanamo: Joint task force for all operations at Guantanamo, formed November 4, 2002.

APPENDIX A

AFGHANISTAN

United States Central Command: One of nine Unified Commands with operational control of U.S. military forces. Area of responsibility includes Afghanistan and Iraq. Commander: Gen. John Abizaid.

Coalition Forces Land Component Command: Senior headquarters element for multi-national land forces in both Iraq and Afghanistan. Commander: Lt. Gen. David McKiernan.

Combined Joint Task Force 180: Forward deployed headquarters for Afghanistan.

IRAQ

United States Central Command.

Coalition Forces Land Component Command.

Combined Joint Task Force 7: Forward deployed headquarters for Operation Iraqi Freedom. Replaced in May 2004 by Multi-National Force—Iraq and Multi-National Corps—Iraq. Commander: Lt. Gen. Ricardo Sanchez.

Combined Joint Task Force 7 C–2: Intelligence staff supporting the task force. Commander: Maj. Gen. Barbara Fast.

800th Military Police Brigade: U.S. Army Reserve Brigade responsible for all internment facilities in Iraq, and assistance to the Coalition Provisional Authority's Minister of Justice. Commander: Brig. Gen. Janis Karpinski.

Joint Interrogation and Detention Center: Element of Combined Joint Task Force 7 for interrogation mission at Abu Ghraib. Commander: Lt. Col. Steven Jordan.

320th Military Police Battalion: Element of 800th Brigade, assigned to Abu Ghraib. Commander: Lt. Col. Jerry Phillabaum.

372nd Military Police Company: Element of the 320th Battalion, assigned to Abu Ghraib in October 2003. Commander: Capt. Donald Reese.

72nd Military Police Company: Nevada National Guard Company, assigned to Abu Ghraib prior to the assignment of the 372nd MP Company.

205th Military Intelligence Brigade: Brigade responsible for multiple Army intelligence missions throughout Iraq. Commander: Col. Thomas Pappas.

519th Military Intelligence Battalion: Tactical exploitation element of the 525th Military Intelligence Brigade; Company A was located at Abu Ghraib. Commander: Maj. Michnewicz.

APPENDIX B:
PRESIDENTIAL MEMO OF FEBRUARY 7, 2002

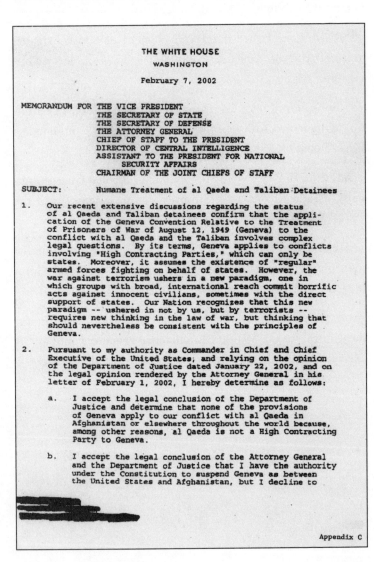

THE WHITE HOUSE

WASHINGTON

February 7, 2002

MEMORANDUM FOR THE VICE PRESIDENT
     THE SECRETARY OF STATE
     THE SECRETARY OF DEFENSE
     THE ATTORNEY GENERAL
     CHIEF OF STAFF TO THE PRESIDENT
     DIRECTOR OF CENTRAL INTELLIGENCE
     ASSISTANT TO THE PRESIDENT FOR NATIONAL
       SECURITY AFFAIRS
     CHAIRMAN OF THE JOINT CHIEFS OF STAFF

SUBJECT: Humane Treatment of al Qaeda and Taliban Detainees

1. Our recent extensive discussions regarding the status
of al Qaeda and Taliban detainees confirm that the application of the Geneva Convention Relative to the Treatment
of Prisoners of War of August 12, 1949 (Geneva) to the
conflict with al Qaeda and the Taliban involves complex
legal questions. By its terms, Geneva applies to conflicts
involving "High Contracting Parties," which can only be
states. Moreover, it assumes the existence of "regular"
armed forces fighting on behalf of states. However, the
war against terrorism ushers in a new paradigm, one in
which groups with broad, international reach commit horrific
acts against innocent civilians, sometimes with the direct
support of states. Our Nation recognizes that this new
paradigm -- ushered in not by us, but by terrorists --
requires new thinking in the law of war, but thinking that
should nevertheless be consistent with the principles of
Geneva.

2. Pursuant to my authority as Commander in Chief and Chief
Executive of the United States; and relying on the opinion
of the Department of Justice dated January 22, 2002, and on
the legal opinion rendered by the Attorney General in his
letter of February 1, 2002, I hereby determine as follows:

  a. I accept the legal conclusion of the Department of
Justice and determine that none of the provisions
of Geneva apply to our conflict with al Qaeda in
Afghanistan or elsewhere throughout the world because,
among other reasons, al Qaeda is not a High Contracting
Party to Geneva.

  b. I accept the legal conclusion of the Attorney General
and the Department of Justice that I have the authority
under the Constitution to suspend Geneva as between
the United States and Afghanistan, but I decline to

2

exercise that authority at this time. Accordingly, I determine that the provisions of Geneva will apply to our present conflict with the Taliban. I reserve the right to exercise this authority in this or future conflicts.

c. I also accept the legal conclusion of the Department of Justice and determine that common Article 3 of Geneva does not apply to either al Qaeda or Taliban detainees, because, among other reasons, the relevant conflicts are international in scope and common Article 3 applies only to "armed conflict not of an international character."

d. Based on the facts supplied by the Department of Defense and the recommendation of the Department of Justice, I determine that the Taliban detainees are unlawful combatants and, therefore, do not qualify as prisoners of war under Article 4 of Geneva. I note that, because Geneva does not apply to our conflict with al Qaeda, al Qaeda detainees also do not qualify as prisoners of war.

3. Of course, our values as a Nation, values that we share with many nations in the world, call for us to treat detainees humanely, including those who are not legally entitled to such treatment. Our Nation has been and will continue to be a strong supporter of Geneva and its principles. As a matter of policy, the United States Armed Forces shall continue to treat detainees humanely and, to the extent appropriate and consistent with military necessity, in a manner consistent with the principles of Geneva.

4. The United States will hold states, organizations, and individuals who gain control of United States personnel responsible for treating such personnel humanely and consistent with applicable law.

5. I hereby reaffirm the order previously issued by the Secretary of Defense to the United States Armed Forces requiring that the detainees be treated humanely and, to the extent appropriate and consistent with military necessity, in a manner consistent with the principles of Geneva.

6. I hereby direct the Secretary of State to communicate my determinations in an appropriate manner to our allies, and other countries and international organizations cooperating in the war against terrorism of global reach.

APPENDIX C:
EVOLUTION OF INTERROGATION TECHNIQUES—GUANTANAMO

Evolution of Interrogation Techniques - GTMO

Interrogation Techniques	FM 34-52 (1992) Jan 02 - 01 Dec 02	Secretary of Defense Approved Tiered System 02 Dec 02 - 15 Jan 03	FM 34-52 (1992) with some 16 Jan 03 - 15 Apr 03 Cat I	Secretary of Defense Memo 16 Apr 03 - Present
Direct questioning	X	X	X	X
Incentive/removal of incentive	X	X	X	X
Emotional love	X	X	X	X
Emotional hate	X	X	X	X
Fear up harsh	X	X	X	X
Fear up mild	X	X	X	X
Reduced fear	X	X	X	X
Pride and ego up	X	X	X	X
Pride and ego down	X	X	X	X
Futility	X	X	X	X
We know all	X	X	X	X
Establish your identity	X	X	X	X
Repetition approach	X	X	X	X
File and dossier	X	X	X	X
Mutt and Jeff		X	X	X*
Rapid Fire	X	X	X	X
Silence	X	X	X	X
Change of Scene	X	X	X	X
Yelling		X (Cat I)	X	X
Deception		X (Cat I)	X	X
Multiple interrogators		X (Cat I)	X	
Interrogator identity		X (Cat I)	X	
Stress positions, like standing		X (Cat II)		
False documents/reports		X (Cat II)		
Isolation for up to 30 days		X (Cat II)		X*
Deprivation of light/auditory stimuli		X (Cat II)		
Hooding (transportation & questioning)		X (Cat II)		
20-interrogations		X (Cat II)		
Removal of ALL comfort items, including religious items		X (Cat II)		
MRE-only diet		X (Cat II)		X*
Removal of clothing		X (Cat II)		
Forced grooming		X (Cat II)		
Exploiting individual phobias, e.g. dogs		X (Cat II)		
Mild, non-injurious physical contact, e.g. grabbing, poking or light pushing		X (Cat III)		
Environmental manipulation				X
Sleep adjustment				X
False flag				X

Also available from PUBLICAFFAIRS REPORTS

Our Plan For America
Stronger at Home, Respected in the World
John Kerry and John Edwards
1-58648-314-5

John Kerry and John Edwards think that America needs more than to get back on course—America needs a whole new direction. And they have a plan to get there. *Our Plan for America*, the official platform of the Kerry campaign, is an essential companion to the issues of today and, if Kerry is elected, an invaluable roadmap to the next four years.

The 9/11 Investigations
Edited by Steven Strasser
1-58648-279-3

"A major, basic reference for anyone who is acutely interested in the events, preludes and aftermath of the September 11, 2001 attacks."
                                        —*The Baltimore Sun*

John F. Kerry
The Complete Biography by the *Boston Globe* Reporters Who
Know Him Best
Michael Kranish, Brian C. Mooney & Nina Easton
1-58648-273-4

"Vigorously researched...a carefully shaded portrait of Mr. Kerry as a man of many contradictions... The voter can only wish that there were as thorough, up-to-date and probing a biography of George W. Bush available before the election."
                                        —*The New York Times*

Also available from

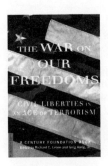

The War on Our Freedoms
Civil Liberties in an Age of Terrorism
Edited by Richard C. Leone & Greg Anrig
1-58648-210-6

"The collateral damage wrought by Mr. Bush's war is not confined to Iraq...*The War on Our Freedoms* is a calmly reasoned report on what the administration has contrived against our liberties in the name of 'homeland security.'"
—Arthur Schlesinger, Jr.

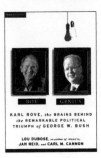

Boy Genius
Karl Rove, the Brains Behind the Remarkable Political Triumph of George W. Bush
Lou Dubose, Jan Reid, and Carl M. Cannon
1-58648-192-4

"A detailed analysis of the strong-arming, grass-roots organizing, and mega-fund raising that Rove masterminded to solidify Bush's power in Washington." —*Austin American-Statesman*

Election 2004:
How Kerry (or Bush) Won and What You Can Expect in the Future
Evan Thomas and the Staff of *Newsweek*
1-58648-293-9

An extraordinary behind-the-scenes look at the 2004 presidential victory—and an insightful glance toward the next four years to come—from the unrivalled political reporters of *Newsweek*.

Available in January 2005

PublicAffairs is a publishing house founded in 1997. It is a tribute to the standards, values, and flair of three persons who have served as mentors to countless reporters, writers, editors, and book people of all kinds, including me.

I.F. STONE, proprietor of *I. F. Stone's Weekly*, combined a commitment to the First Amendment with entrepreneurial zeal and reporting skill and became one of the great independent journalists in American history. At the age of eighty, Izzy published *The Trial of Socrates,* which was a national bestseller. He wrote the book after he taught himself ancient Greek.

BENJAMIN C. BRADLEE was for nearly thirty years the charismatic editorial leader of *The Washington Post*. It was Ben who gave the *Post* the range and courage to pursue such historic issues as Watergate. He supported his reporters with a tenacity that made them fearless and it is no accident that so many became authors of influential, best-selling books.

ROBERT L. BERNSTEIN, the chief executive of Random House for more than a quarter century, guided one of the nation's premier publishing houses. Bob was personally responsible for many books of political dissent and argument that challenged tyranny around the globe. He is also the founder and longtime chair of Human Rights Watch, one of the most respected human rights organizations in the world.

For fifty years, the banner of Public Affairs Press was carried by its owner Morris B. Schnapper, who published Gandhi, Nasser, Toynbee, Truman and about 1,500 other authors. In 1983, Schnapper was described by *The Washington Post* as "a redoubtable gadfly." His legacy will endure in the books to come.

Peter Osnos, *Publisher*